W9-CMD-200

Also by Rob Schultheis

THE HIDDEN WEST

BONE
GAMES

Rob Schultheis

BONE GAMES

One Man's Search
for the Ultimate
Athletic High

Fromm International Publishing Corporation

NEW YORK

Published in 1986 by
Fromm International Publishing Corporation
560 Lexington Avenue
New York, N.Y. 10022

Published by arrangement with Random House, Inc.
BONE GAMES: *One Man's Search for the Ultimate Athletic High.*
Copyright © 1984 by Rob Schultheis.
All rights reserved under International and Pan-American
Copyright conventions. Published in the United States
by Random House, Inc., New York and simultaneously
in Canada by Random House of Canada Limited, Toronto.

Printed in the United States of America.

Grateful acknowledgement is made to the following
for permission to reprint previously
published material:

The American Alpine Club: quotation by
Yvon Chounard reprinted from *The American
Journal* by permission of the American
Alpine Club.

Random House, Inc.: an excerpt from "The Lay
of the Luckless Mountaineers." From *Mount
Analogue* by Rene Daumal, translated by Roger
Shattuck. Copyright © 1959 by Vincent Stuart,
Ltd. Reprinted by permission of Pantheon Books,
a division of Random House, Inc.

Ray Smutke: excerpt from Albert St. Gallen Heims'
Remarks on Fatal Falls, as translated and quoted
by Mike Quigley in "Falling," *Off Belay* Magazine,
October 1975. Copyright © 1975 by
Off Belay Magazine.

Library of Congress Cataloging in Publication Data

Schultheis, Rob.
Bone games.

Reprint. Originally published: New York:
Random House, 1984.

1. Sports—Psychological aspects. I. Title.

[GV706.4.S35 1986] 796'.01 85-29363
ISBN 0-88064-058-8 (pbk.)

To Alexandra

BONE
GAMES

1

In 1964 I fell off a mountain in the Colorado Rockies and came within a few inches of dying. The mountain's name was Neva, from the French *névé,* "field of granular snow"; its summit was only 12,814 feet above sea level. There are fifty-two peaks over 14,000 feet in Colorado, and literally hundreds over 12,500. Neva was an insignificant place, really, not the kind of place you would expect to meet up with death.

I had started out from Boulder, at the edge of the Great Plains, on a hot and dusty morning; hitched a ride up Boulder Canyon to the shacktown of Nederland, and another ride on the dirt road into Fourth of July Valley, through pine and aspen forests. The snow peaks of the Great Divide, which separates the Pacific and Atlantic watersheds, gleamed to the west. Two raindrops could fall an inch apart, up on those lonesome summits, and one end up in the Colorado River, rolling through the bedrock cellar of Utah, the other in the North Platte, riding east across the prairies to the Missouri, the Mississippi, south to the Gulf of Mexico: in both cases a long, wild way to go.

My second ride was with an old doctor from Denver, who stopped to fly-fish the stream beside the road; I hiked on, my pack on my back, using my ice ax as a walking stick. It was a long, drowsy June afternoon: in the open meadows it felt like midsummer, but where the road ran through the deep timber it was chill; the black humus smelled of ghosts. As I went higher, the road ran with ribbons of meltwater from the snows above. The air had that burnt thinness that comes with altitude.

In the late afternoon I came to the end of the road. There was an abandoned mine shack by the creek, with a vandalized cast-iron stove, a skeletal mattress on a bed frame. I set up camp there as the sun went down: filled my water bottle from the stream, unrolled my army surplus duck-feather sleeping bag ($25 on Larimer Street in Denver), lit a candle. Dinner was black bread, cheese, a compressed meat bar, and instant coffee heated on a Sterno stove. The first stars shone through the shattered windows. The air grew frigid.

I crawled into my bag and huddled up on my side. The planks of the cabin floor radiated cold, cold that sliced through the thin sleeping bag, my cheap synthetic parka and sweater. It was like sleeping on a marble floor in the Throne Room of the Mountain King. Sleep was difficult: I tossed and turned, dreams banging around in my skull like bobsleds.

When I woke, the pinetops were already red with morning. I ate more black bread and an orange, cached my gear in a thicket, and headed up the trail with my ice ax in my hand, my crampons slung over my shoulder, United States Geological Survey map folded up in my pocket.

The snow was deep on the high country that year. The trail switch-backed up through the timber, ponderosa pine and Douglas fir. I found myself stamping over dunes of hard old snow, four, five, six feet thick; down under, I could hear the meltwater running, and here and there were patches of earth, black as tar, studded with green shoots. After a steep couple of miles the forest thinned; I crossed into the alpine zone, wind-twisted dwarf juniper, sodden hummocks of grass, boulders splashed with lichens, inlaid with moss. Snow, snow, and more snow. To the left, Fourth of July Valley fell away into empty space, with the snowed-up timber of the valley floor far, far below; beyond, more jagged peaks rose. To my right, the massive hulk of Arapaho Peak blocked off half the sky; it blazed in the sun like a pyramid of molten glass. Ahead, higher, was the Divide, Mount Neva.

The trail wound up, traversing loose screes and fields of ossified snow. It was hot, clear, the sky so blue it seemed almost black. The landscape pounded in my eyes. Nothing moved all across this vast world, where I toiled like an insect through the immense debris of dead mountains, ancient storms.

It must have been late morning—I didn't own a watch, thought I was immune to time, back then—when I reached the northeast buttresses of Neva and turned south, across the bowl-like cirque valley at the base of the mountain. More snow here: there was a lake, called Dorothy on the map, buried beneath the snow and ice. Somewhere down there trout drifted in the utter blackness; what worlds revolved in those blind silver heads? I could not see the summit of Neva now; the angle of the peak's east face cut it off.

It took me till sometime in the early afternoon to climb
the face, cutting steps in the granular snow, digging in with
my cramponed boots. There was only one really tricky point
in the ascent, where the snowfields ended in a series of
broken ledges. I had to clamber up over the rotten rock
with six hundred feet of sky at my back, clinging to loose
flakes with my fingers, iron crampon points skidding on the
stone. Nasty work. I have always been afflicted with vertigo,
and it hit me now, roaring in my ears as if I were underwater,
unstringing my nerve. I clung to the mountain like a lover,
a lover whose loved one is about to leave him forever. I
wanted to melt into the safety of the stone. Somehow I
forced my body away from the mountainside, reconnected
my hands and feet, and muscled up over the last ledges, onto
the scree slope that led to the summit. Boulders, cobbles,
shingles of granite, hanging in suspended animation in the
void; years later, Tom Quinn would tell me how he and
Layton Korr were just missed by a falling rock the size of
a telephone booth, on this same remote face. I trudged up
that last stone staircase until it ended—the summit, the end.

While I had been climbing, the weather had been changing, the way mountain weather does, swiftly and without
warning. When I looked away from the summit, the sky
was blackening to the north and south, along the peaks of
the Divide. Out to the west, toward Grand Lake, the rolling
timber dimmed out in shrouds of mist. Storm clouds rumbled
across Fourth of July Valley; in the distance a sound like
blocks of stone being sledgehammered, a sizzle of lightning.
The air turned cold and hard, and pellets of grapeshot hurtled
in on the wind, hissing across the granite slats of the summit.
It had been July, climbing on those sunny snow slopes below: air almost balmy, the cloudless light bombarding off

the white mountainside . . . Now, like magic, it was late
November, and December coming on hard. Drastic magic,
indeed.

I heard a sound like a million bees buzzing, and smelled
scorched ions on the air. I could almost see the electricity
waltzing in the air around me, enough of it to strike me dead
a thousand times over. The blade of my ice ax spat like an
adder. I had taken my crampons off and hung them over my
shoulder again; now the sharp points, stabbing into my back
through the sweater and shirt, began to give off tiny electrical
shocks. I felt like a skin diver held in the jaws of a giant
shark; it would either spit me out or chew me into bits, and
there was nothing I could do about it, nothing at all.

It was time to move on, fast. According to the Geological
Survey map, Neva's ridgeline led north, eventually descending, after various zigs and zags, ups and downs, to the trail
across Fourth of July Pass, the same trail I had come up that
morning. It looked dodgy, on the map, and the little part
of it visible from where I stood: anyone in his right mind,
with a grain of sense, would have turned and gone down
the same way he had come up. Down-climbing is .hard
enough without throwing absolute ignorance of the terrain
into the equation. Once I made it down through the ledges,
I would have found that perfect ladder of ax-hewn holds,
left by me on my ascent, leading back down into the cirque.
But I was not in my right mind that day; I had left logic
far behind. Possessed by something between panic and
euphoria, dread and ecstasy, I began to traverse the ridge to
the north—down the rubble of the summit, and out onto the
ridgeline itself, a chockablock junk heap of granite. Clouds
swirled below; here and there peaks stood up like tusks in
the queer fluorescent light. The summit vanished in cloud

behind me. I scuttled across a series of slabs and into a sawtooth of crags. The ridge grew narrower, more severe, the rock dusted with new snow, slick as a whistle.

To my right, everything fell away into nothing: I stared down vertical buttresses that glinted like steel. Much harder than anything I had climbed in my three months of rock-climbing experience: impossible. I remembered something Nietzsche wrote, about staring into the abyss and discovering that it is staring back into you. I felt the whole sky in my throat; it felt like I was already falling, had always been falling, through heavens of my own dreaming. Death's Black Caress, someone once called it. My fingers looked suddenly pitiful, shrunken, and withered against the indomitable stone. I was a sack of winds, a tuneless bagpipe, tied to a rack of creaking bones. *Steady,* I told myself. *Slow down. Don't blow it now. In an hour, maybe less, you'll be walking down that trail, safe and sound . . .*

To the left, west, a confusion of steep rock and wind-scoured snow descended precipitously to a sepulchral chasm, the Land of the Dead. Ice ax and crampons jangled on my back as I picked my way between nothingness and nothing-ness. I once read of an extremely theoretical physicist who studied matter and decided it was so close to being non-existent, unstable, perforated, insubstantial, that he began wearing giant clown's shoes on campus so he wouldn't slip through the crust of the earth. I knew exactly how he felt. There seemed to be nothing I could depend on anywhere.

If I could just descend twenty or thirty feet to the west, I thought, the going would be easier; there would be a ledge, a track, *something*—a way to the north, off that tenuous zone. I had no reason for my faith: I wanted it to be so, and in some childish way I thought wanting would make it so.

I began to down-climb an overhanging crevice toward what looked like a way, something. Midway down, there was a foothold I had to stretch for. I hung from my handhold, a big spur of rock, with both hands, and let myself down slowly until my arms were stretched to the limit. I swung my right boot over onto the hold, but when I began to rest my weight on it, skidded off. The rock was covered with a thin skin of ice. I tried to balance on it again, but it was impossible. No go there.

I hung there for I don't know how long: thirty seconds, two minutes, half an hour. I couldn't climb back up the overhanging rock, and I could not descend; there was no egress to either side. *Gripped*, as climbers say: in the grip of panic, terror, frozen stiff. I still had some vague, fey idea that I was at least partially in control of the situation; that I could drop, with the sureness of a cat, and catch myself on the steep mountainside below. I was quite crazy, of course. The blood drained from my arms; my fingers went dead. Finally, without meaning to, I let go.

I hurtled down, slamming against the rock wall; my knee cracked hard, and I grabbed wildly for something to break my fall. The world spun like a top. I hit again, and again: no pain, just a jolt, but I knew, on some rapid-fire subconscious level, I was being injured. Suddenly it all stopped: I was lying on a narrow, sloping ledge; my head lay next to the emptiness, and I was staring down into at least two hundred feet of thin air. A few more inches, and I would have plummeted on down to my death on the cruel rocks. They weren't really cruel, of course—if they had any thoughts at all, they were the slow, gentle ones I imagine rocks must have—but they looked cruel to me. Beyond were horse-white fields of snow and more steep rocks, leading down to a dead-end chasm. I hated it all, feared and hated it: there was a razor up those granite sleeves, I thought, and a killer's snicker on the wind . . . I was terrified, and my terror made me furious at what I feared.

It took me a long, long time, but slowly, painfully, I put together the elaborate series of moves that got me up on my knees. It was incredibly complicated, like building a scale model of the Taj Mahal out of toothpicks. I was beginning to realize what bad shape I was in. My ice ax (it was stuck in the rocks just above the ledge) had thrashed my legs somewhere in mid-fall; blood seeped through my pants, blotches on my knees the size of waterlilies. I had fallen on my crampons, stabbing myself in the back with the dozen tiny dagger points. I stared aghast down the huge, tilted desert of Neva's western face. Somehow I had to cross that forbidden terrain and then find a way out of the chasm below, back over the mountain wall to the shack where I had camped. What time was it? Past three and fading fast. There was no shelter here; if I didn't escape by nightfall, I wouldn't survive till morning.

Tears were running down my face; I wept like a small boy, with fear, hurt, and the shame of being injured. I wanted someone to take me by the hand and lead me home, but that's not the way it works. I was on my own, alone. I got to my feet, retrieved my ice ax and crampons, strung them on my back, and like a sleepwalker began to make my way down the precipice.

Something happened on that descent, something I have tried to figure out ever since, so inexplicable and powerful it was. I found myself very simply doing impossible things: dozens, scores of them, as I down-climbed Neva's lethal slopes. Shattered, in shock, I climbed with the impeccable sureness of a snow leopard, a mountain goat. I crossed disintegrating chutes of rock holds vanishing from under my hands and feet as I moved, a dance in which a single missed beat would have been fatal. I used bits of rime clinging to the granite as fingerholds. They rattled away into space but I was already gone, away. Tatters of cloud drifted over me, rubbed up against me like cats; I could feel the static in them, throbbing. It was drizzling sleet to the west, misting where I was; the rocks gleamed damp. *What I am doing is absolutely impossible,* I thought. *I can't be doing this. But I have the grace, the radiant mojo, and here I am!*

In one spot, the only way down was a pillar of black water ice: I shinnied down it, hands jammed between the ice and the rock face, boot heels jammed against the mountain, toes against the tissue-thin ripples in the great icicle's flank. Impossible, absurd. Then a vertical pitch of rock, nothing to hold on to and fifteen feet of it, and I clung to the *grain of the granite*—no, but I did—and moved down over it, onto more ice-scoured ledges. Talk about dodging bullets: this was like dodging a Gatling gun in a broom closet. Gravity lunged to take me; I leapt aside, again and again. All the days I had spent rock-climbing in the hills above Boulder, I had never done anything one half, one tenth this hard; I knew my limitations, and I was climbing way, way beyond them. One small part of me trembled with fear and fatigue, cried out to be rescued, to be whisked away to any place other than this bleak precipice. The rest, confident, full of an unsane joy, reveled in the animal dance of survival, admired the brilliant crystals in the granite, the drunken calligraphy of ice crystals . . . was totally possessed by the act of mountaineering, by the mountain, rejoiced in the immense vertigo of the place. It was like certain dreams I have had in which my body is as light as a feather, lighter, and I leap off one foot, effortlessly, and drift ten, twenty, thirty feet into the air; with a flick of one wrist I set myself spinning like a top.

Looking back on it, I really cannot explain or describe properly that strange person I found inhabiting my body that afternoon. It was just too different from my everyday self, and I have never seen its like before, nor have I seen it since, except for a split second in Mexico in 1982, and a few strange weeks of long-distance running . . . more on that later. The person I became on Neva was the best possible version of myself, the person I *should have been* throughout my life. No regrets, no hesitation; there were no false moves left in me. I really believe I could have hit a mosquito in the eye with a pine needle at thirty paces; I couldn't miss because there was no such thing as a miss. It didn't matter whether I fell or not, because I could not fall, any more than two plus two can equal three. It was all sublime nonsense, of course, but I believed it, down in my very cells; if I hadn't believed, I would have been hurled into the Pit below.

Some time after, I found myself trudging through the deep snowdrifts at the base of the mountain. The storm had broken, and the chasm was full of a tremendous light. Streamers of cloud raced across the sky. The ridges looked like they were chiseled out of fire opal.

I hiked north, paralleling the Divide, postholing through the snow up to my knees every few steps; I struggled back onto the frozen crust on my hands and knees, got to my feet, and soldiered on. According to the map, there was a trail down there somewhere, the trail that led east, back over Fourth of July Pass, back down to the shack where I had camped; a long, long way to go, but I had no choice. I kept marching, kept falling, picking myself up again. The snow thinned and I was on the screes, slogging up the cobble-stones of Neva's northwestern corner. When I saw the trail, a vague line climbing east, toward the invisible pass, it seemed like a path in a fairy tale leading from one world into another.

It was a long climb to the top of the pass. The light changed as the afternoon began to wane. The summit was a boulder field with pockets of gravelly soil, tufts of dry grass bronzed by the late sun. On my left, a snowfield dropped into the ghastly depths of the Hellhole, under Arapaho Peak. The trail led east, down to the shack and on down to Boulder, the Great Plains, the world. And I was on the trail; it was all downhill from here. It all lay before me. I felt I could pick it up, the whole world, like a golden apple. My old life, everything before that moment I had let go of the rock and fallen, was gone. It had been a dry, cramped husk anyway; I watched it blow away without a bit of regret. Joy filled me, from the soles of my feet to the tips of the hairs on my head.

You have to be as cautious as a wild animal or a guerrilla in this world: your revelations slip away from you before you know it. So it was with that dose of enlightenment, what Zen Buddhism calls *satori*, on Neva. I had tasted a hit of enlightenment, perfection, Buddha Nature, godhead, what-ever . . . What's in a name, anyway? By nightfall, as I reached the cabin, I was beginning to slip back into my old self again.

I spent the night in the mine shack, and hiked, limping, out the valley the next morning, and hitched a ride back down to Boulder. I spent the next two days in bed, in my rented room on Arapaho Street, sliding in and out of a death-like sleep. My whole body felt as if it had been beaten, bruised to the very bone. There was a mysterious slash across my shoulder blades; my fingertips were cloudy, black, numb. I could barely bend my left elbow. There was a buzzing in my ears; the walls of the room wobbled like aspic.

On the third day after my return, I hobbled up to the university cafeteria and ate a cheeseburger and a piece of pie. Afterwards I lay on the lawn in front of the library, in the sun. The strength was flowing back into me, and with it, my everyday, screwed-up life. Interesting, but it seemed that my uncanny power on Neva had sprung from the absolute desperation and helplessness of my situation there: as if we need to be emptied out, bled of everything, before the gods condescend to fill us with their own brand of grace.

In the next few weeks I fell in and out of love, and halfway in again. I traveled back to the East Coast, I got a summer job, I planned my fall college courses. The magic from the mountain was gone. In the autumn I returned to Colorado and began to study for a degree in anthropology.

In a subtle way, though, that climb and fall stayed with me; it took the form of a sense of loss, an area of hunger deep inside.

Imagine that someone, a terrible wizard, gave you a potion that made everything perfect for a few hours; you knew everything, you could do anything, all your dreams come true. Then the potion wore off, and you found yourself back in your old, tired-out body, with your old, ignorant mind. The wizard has gone away, no one knows where, taking his potions with him. You had tasted heaven; now you were stuck back on earth, with no sign of redemption.

That was how I felt; and looking back on it now, I am not sure if that tantalizing bit of nirvana on Mount Neva was a blessing or a curse.

2

I wanted to find my way back to that supernal state I had literally fallen into on Mount Neva; I wanted to trace a map of that inner space of 100 percent awareness and poise, beside which the rest of my life was like a muffled, mummified, musty daydream, a case of endless low-grade spiritual influenza.

It seemed to me that the possibilities and potentialities were tremendously exciting. What, I asked myself, if one could tap into that tremendous energy at will, or even just more often, both in and out of games? Too much Nietzsche on the brain, perhaps, but I couldn't let the idea go. I imagined a kind of Zen *Uebermensch*, senses keyed to the absolute optimum, equilibrium of an archangel, dancing through life with the greatest of ease . . . too much Carlos Castaneda/Don Juan on the brain, too, perhaps: every man a shaman, and God talking to all. But how could I deny the power, and the authenticity, of what had happened to me up

there? I had had It, that nameless unthing that once caused
Lewis Carroll to write:

> Where life becomes a Spasm,
> And History a Whiz:
> If that is not Sensation,
> I don't know what it is.

Had had It, and wanted It again. What made it incredibly
tantalizing was that It, the magic, was somewhere inside me;
It had always been there, I felt, and It always would be
until the day I died: dormant, waiting to be awakened by
an instant of panic, danger, total desperation.

Well, I thought, I would find a way of awakening it again
and grasping it, using it, or I would try to, anyway. It was
a search well worth the effort. My body and mind seemed
to me to be like the New World in 1491: a whole lost
continent of unknown treasures, waiting to be explored,
charted, brought to light. There were many potential maps,
of course—physiological, psychological, biochemical, theological, and anthropological, to name a few; I would run
through them all, and more if necessary, till I found the
right one or ones: till I found the way back.

I began to look for clues in the most obvious place, the
experiences of other adventurers and extreme athletes. If
risk and stress had squeezed a kind of satori out of me on
Neva, it stood to reason others had had the same kind of
experience in similar circumstances; and if they had, perhaps by examining them case by case I might be able to put
together an etiology of stress-triggered peak performance and
ecstasy: a grammar of abracadabra.

As it turned out, there were plenty of cases similar to mine. John Muir, for instance: the great pioneer backwoodsman and naturalist was solo-climbing Mount Ritter, in the Sierra Nevada, when he found himself stranded high on a cliff face. Unable to move up or down, frozen with terror, "I seemed suddenly to become possessed of a new sense," Muir recollected later. "The other self, bygone experience, Instinct, or Guardian Angel—call it what you will—came forward and assumed control. Then my trembling became firm again, every rift and flaw [in the rock] was seen as through a microscope, and my limbs moved with a positiveness and a precision with which I seemed to have nothing at all to do. Had I been borne aloft upon wings, my deliverance could not have been more complete." He climbed to the top with unbelievable ease.

The Swiss geologist Albert von St. Gallen Heim collected dozens of similar accounts in his eccentric 1892 monograph, *Remarks on Fatal Falls (Notizen über dem Tod durch Absturz)*. In interviews with survivors of climbing falls and other accidents, St. Gallen Heim concluded that "there was no anxiety, no trace of despair, no pain. . . . Mental activity became enormous, rising to a hundredfold velocity or intensity. The relationship of events and their probable outcomes were overviewed with objective clarity. . . . The individual acted with lightning quickness." St. Gallen Heim himself survived a fall beneath a speeding wagon by choreographing a series of split-second moves he could only wonder at afterwards:

The following series of thoughts went through my mind: I cannot manage to hold on [to the side of the wagon] until the horse comes to a stop. I must let go. I will fall on my back and the wheel will be unavoidable. I must fall upon my stomach and the wheel will pass over the backs of my legs. If I will tense the muscles, they will be a protective cushion for the bones. The pressure of the street will be somewhat less likely to break a bone than the pressure of the wheel. If I am able to turn myself to the left, then perhaps I can sufficiently draw back my left leg. On the other hand, turning to the right would, by the dimensions of the wagon, result in both legs being broken under it.

Thereupon, through a jerk of my arm, I turned myself to the left, swung my left leg powerfully outward and simultaneously tensed my leg muscles to the limit of their strength. The wheel passed over my right ham, and I came out of it with a slight bruise.

I know quite clearly that I let myself fall only after these lightning fast, wholly precise reflections, which seemed to imprint themselves upon my brain.

Charles Lindbergh, fighting to stay awake during his 1926 solo flight from New York to Paris, was visited by a kind of personified version of stress-induced strength; he described this almost supernatural visitation in detail in his book *The Spirit of St. Louis*:

While I'm staring at the instruments, during an unearthly age of time, both conscious and asleep, the fuselage behind me becomes filled with ghostly presences—vaguely outlined forms, transparent, moving, riding weightless with me in the plane. I feel no surprise at their coming. . . . Without turning my head, I see them as clearly as though in my normal field of vision. There's no limit to my sight.

These "friendly vaporlike shapes . . . emanations from the experience of ages, inhabitants of a universe closed to mortal men," as Lindbergh described them, spoke to Lindbergh, helping him with his navigation, giving him "messages of importance unattainable in ordinary life." Lindbergh felt his own body dissolve in the presence of the spirits; he felt invulnerable, transfused with their intangible power. The unearthly phantoms helped the young pilot through the worst part of his flight, the dark night of both body and soul, and then dissolved away into air.

Athletes and adventurers have been stumbling on these kinds of mystical experiences for years, but it wasn't until the 1960s and 70s that a few hard-core runners, climbers, kayakers, surfers, hang glider flyers, and skiers, most of them in the American West, began deliberately to search out power in their games. Many of these athletic vision seekers were veterans of the LSD and Eastern guru movements; they discovered that the same highs drugs and meditation gave you were available in extreme sports, only in a more profound and stable form. In an article titled "The Climber as Visionary," in the May 1969 issue of *Ascent*, the California mountaineers Doug Robinson wrote, "A young climber begins to find parallels between the visionary results of his climbing discipline and his formerly inaccessible visionary life in the acid subculture." He went on to quote fellow climber Yvon Chouinard's account of an eight-day climb of El Capitan, in Yosemite:

. . . we now appreciated everything around us. Each individual crystal in the granite stood out in bold relief. The varied shapes of the clouds never ceased to attract attention. For the first time we noticed tiny bugs that were all over the walls, so tiny they were barely noticeable. While belaying, I stared at one for fifteen minutes, watching him move and admiring his brilliant red color. How could one ever be bored with so many good things to see and feel? This unity with our joyous surroundings, this ultra penetrating perception, gave us a feeling of contentment that we had not had for years.

"Chouinard's vision was no accident," Robinson concluded. "It was the result of days of climbing. He was tempered by technical difficulties, dehydration, striving, the sensory desert, weariness, the gradual loss of self."

Some skiers discovered the same kind of stress-triggered ecstasy in their own sport. Gil Harrison, a top U.S. ski racer in the 1960s and later a ski patrolman, Hindu meditator, and ranch-hand, described the rush he got from downhill racing: "When those gates and bumps are whizzing by and the wind is howling through your crash helmet, there's no time to think about anything—I always forgot to breathe—so right away you're in another world, de facto, thinkless, sensual perceptions leaping out at you, vision narrowed to one-pointedness. And then the finish gate, and the wind stops, and you're back. But you're still high, and you know that brighter, more intense world is still out there."

And Rick Trujillo, the great long-distance high-altitude runner, a sleek lanky man who looks like he was sculpted in a wind tunnel; the same brand of revelation and power from games pushed to the nth power.

Born into an old-time Hispanic hard-rock mining family in the little Colorado alpine town of Ouray (741 population, 9,500 feet above sea level), Trujillo got into running when he was fifteen, with the Ouray High School track team. "It was a snowstorm in March, typical spring weather around here. The snow was waist-deep when we got up into the canyon, and we almost froze. We ended up staggering back down into town, completely exhausted, but I knew right then that I enjoyed running. School ended, summer came, and I just kept on running. I've been running ever since."

Trujillo went on to the University of Colorado, where he majored in geology and competed on the cross-country team. He never really cared for flatland running, though, and he found intercollegiate training and competition a grind: "I got tired of running the same miles over and over, fighting dogs, traffic and people." Also, to tell the truth of it, Trujillo was less than spectacular as a non-mountain runner: he dropped out of the only two regulation marathons he entered, complaining that the flat terrain and pavement hurt his knees and ankles, blistered his feet.

Mountain running was a different story: on steep ground in thin air, Trujillo was well-nigh unbeatable at the peak of his career. His favorite race was the Pikes Peak, an arduous event held every summer in the mountains behind Colorado Springs. The 28.3-mile course begins in the suburb of Manitou Springs, winds via forest and scree slope 7,748 vertical feet to the 14,110-foot summit of Pikes, and retraces the same route to the base of the mountain. Trujillo won the Pikes Peak five years in a row, between 1972 and 1977, beating mountain running stars like the champion Scottish fell runner* Jos Naylor in the process. His fastest time for the course, 3:34:15, set in 1976, would be a creditable time for a 26.2-mile marathon on level ground at sea level; for 28 plus miles on a 14,000-footer, it is in the realm of dreams.

---

* Fell running is a peculiarly Scottish sport that involves racing from summit to summit over the moors in the vilest weather. Races often extend into the night, adding to the hazards of cold, fog, cliff, and quarry.

But it is Trujillo's noncompetitive running that is really interesting, in the context of athletic mysticism. Rick now lives back in Ouray, where he works as a mining geologist, and he has developed a whole series of what he calls "H, T and E runs"—"here, there and everywhere"—in the surrounding mountains. The Imogene Pass jeep road from Ouray to Telluride, for instance: 18 miles of dirt switchbacks, climbing 5,300 feet to a 13,114-foot pass, then descending 4,500 vertical feet into the town of Telluride. There is an annual race over the pass, attracting scores of serious high-altitude runners, but Trujillo prefers to run it alone, after a day's work at the mine. He tanks up on his favorite running fuel, chocolate chip cookies, and then heads up out of Ouray's valley, up through the darkening woods, crossing the summit rockfields as the sun sets, alpenglow flashing on the peaks of the San Juan Range, Mendota, Greenback, Snaeffels, Ajax . . . Descends to Telluride in the last vestiges of light, loping down past the great waterfalls, through the ruins of mining camps . . . Hitchhikes home in time for a late dinner. He has been known to do the run in under two and a half hours.

Imogene is about as tame as Trujillo's runs get. Another favorite one follows the Twin Peaks Trail above Ouray, climbing 3,000 vertical feet in 3 miles; the last mile is a 3½ to 1 (30 percent) grade of unstable dirt and loose rock. In winter, when the trails and back roads are too heavily snowed up to run, Rick takes to U.S. 550, the so-called Million-Dollar Highway, that runs south from Ouray over a series of avalanche-bombed passes. He describes the hazards of the road as if they are marvelous: "There is everything from avalanches to rock falls to almost running over cliffs in the dark. Once I was running down by the Bear Creek Falls, slipped on some ice, slid about forty feet and almost went over the edge. There's no guardrail there, and it's about four hundred feet down.

"Then there's the Ruby Cliffs above town. Rocks and ice are coming off there all the time. You stay on the outside of the road so you can hear the rocks and ice coming down, and at least you can tell which way to dodge. The Mother Cline Slide has almost gotten me a couple of times . . . And I've seen the East Riverside Slide run several times in the spring."

To Trujillo, solo mountain running is the ultimate. "Ninety-nine point nine percent of my running has been by myself," he says, "and that's all right with me . . . Cliff-climbing, steep grades, going up and down. You can't stop and think. Your eyes see what's in front of you and your legs and feet just follow. You are aware of what's in front of you, but you don't think, This foot goes here and that foot goes there. Things happen too fast."

He goes on to tell of a run he did a few years back, in a high valley above Ouray. He happened on a herd of elk; they spooked and clambered up a hill and through a stand of thick aspens to get away. Trujillo followed, loping along, keeping pace with them. They ran farther; he stayed on their trail. For three, four hours he followed the herd; slowly the boundaries between them melted. "Up and down, over logs and rocks, down creek beds, through brush alder and dead-fall . . . I started out chasing them, but in the end we were running together. I felt like I could run forever."

Modern kayakers and canoeists have also used their sport, pushed to the limit, to find transcendent experiences. In one of the most interesting cases, an anonymous kayaker ran the Grand Canyon of the Colorado alone, illegally, during the winter of 1977–78—the cold off-season when few people visit the river; he later published an account of the trip under the title "The Big Sneak," in the obscure journal *Mountain Gazette*. Anonymous's journey was really drastic. The weather was foul, the river cold enough to induce hypothermia after less than a minute's immersion; aiming to set a solo speed record for running the canyon, the lone extremist paddled until his muscles were knotted up in agony, and choked down freeze-dried food in raw powder form to save the time it would have taken to cook it. Perfect vision conditions. Exhausted, half frozen, in the dark depths of the gorge, he saw the ghost of the great whitewaterman Walter Kirschbaum, in an antique kayak, talking to the ghost of the classic mountaineer George Herbert Leigh-Mallory, standing on the riverbank . . . "They speak quietly just above a whisper, and seem to be referring to me as a protégé of the man in the boat. Straining to catch their conversation, I am humbled to hear him remark, 'Doesn't look like such a hard man now . . .' 'So little of that sort of thing these days . . .' replies the man on the shore." Like Lindbergh's cockpit angels, the two figures in the canyon seemed to transmit strength and nerve into the desperate kayaker, helping him finish his trip successfully.

Dr. Hannes Lindemann, an eccentric German tropical medicine specialist, did two remarkable voyages during the fifties that took him into visionary territory. The first, in 1955, a transatlantic solo in a 24-foot dugout canoe, was not written up in English, but the journal of his 72-day crossing in a 17-foot foldboat (!) two years later appeared in the July 22, 1957, *Life*. Lindemann's collapsible canvas boat began to leak the second day out from the Canaries; he was allergic to the craft's waterproofing compound, making his

whole body burn "as if hot tar had been poured over it."
Dead calms were followed by monster storms (Lindemann
did his crossing in autumn/winter, a particularly hazardous
climatic season in the mid-Atlantic).

By the two-thirds point in the voyage, the isolation and
pain were compounded by sleeplessness: Lindemann could
seldom doze off for more than a half hour at a time because
of the difficulty of navigating and maneuvering the dodgy
foldboat through heavy seas. The doctor began to hear voices,
auditory hallucinations, urging him subtly on his way. "Again
I heard voices, so I answered and spoke everything as if to
friends: 'Where is the knife?' 'Not here.' 'Come on, here is
some work for you.'" Eventually the voices solidified into a
small black boy, a hallucination that coalesced out of the
black rubber outrigger during particularly difficult times,
engaging Lindemann in long, encouraging conversations. In
one incident, Lindemann asked his incorporeal companion,
"Boy, where are your employers living?" "In the West," the
boy replied. *West!* Lindemann suddenly leapt back into consciousness, sensing somehow that he was off course; he looked
at his compass and found that he had indeed drifted off his
westward line toward the New World.

In an interesting parallel incident, Captain Joshua Slocum,
sailing alone around the world at the turn of the century, was
struck down by a fever during a spell of rough weather in
the mid-Atlantic. Stretched out on his bunk, half delirious,
Slocum was visited by an apparition, the ghost of Christopher
Columbus's navigator. The ghostly figure told him not to
worry: that he, the wise spirit, would hold the little boat on
course through the night. When Slocum awoke the next
day and checked his position, he found he was still, miracu-
lously, sailing dead true toward his destination.

The kayakers and canoeists of the Washington, D.C., area, among the finest in the world, tell many stories of "breaking through" in the throes of their sport.

"Whitewater blows all your synapses clean," says Pope Barrow, a deceptively quiet-looking young Capitol Hill attorney who has been canoeing and kayaking rapids for eleven years. He talks about going up to the Great Falls of the Potomac one time in midwinter, when 90 percent of the rapids were iced over, trying to find one or two tiny chutes of open water to run. (The Great Falls are huge and violent; during flood season their flow rivals that of Niagara.) Pope's companion, whose idea the winter outing was, broke through the ice, and ended up hanging from his kayak, which was jammed across the hole, suspended over the boiling rapids. Somehow he climbed to safety, while Pope crossed the same thin ice by sitting on his kayak and using it to support his weight while he eased himself across. Other runs were, are, even dicier: Tom Yanosky, for instance, took an open-deck fifteen-foot canoe down the Potomac River below Great Falls at the height of Hurricane Agnes, in 1972, when the river was running at 350,000 cubic feet per second, a hundred times its normal flow. The waves topped out at over twelve feet, and huge pieces of floating debris, including a hundred-foot-high uprooted maple tree, threatened to crush Tom and his boat; below the Cabin John Bridge, he barely escaped being sucked under by a series of giant whirlpools. To this day, Yanosky's Agnes voyage remains the pivotal event in his life, "the most important thing I've ever done," in his own words.

Barrow himself likes to seek out situations where the water conditions and his level of skill interlock in a state of perfect dynamic tension: "One of the times I deliberately

went at or over my limit was in Tumwear Canyon on the
Wenatchee River in Washington State . . . I was out there
with two friends, one from Alaska and one from D.C. who's
a coach of the U.S. Whitewater Team. Jack, the guy from
Alaska, is no great paddler, but he'll try anything, even if
he gets demolished. He's one of the only people to do the
Susitna River: he got as far as Devil's Canyon and found
out it was Trash City, so he left his kayak on the banks,
climbed up the cliffs, and walked forty miles to Talkeetna.
No one else did the river for the next six years—and then
it was Walt Blackadar, they were going to do this big television spectacular, and the first thing they found was Jack's
boat, still there!"

Jack dislocated his shoulder on the Wenatchee; then
Gordon, the whitewater coach, decided that Tumwear was
just too much for him. Barrow went on alone.

"I spent two hours scouting this canyon from the highway
above. It was really an unnatural kind of place—continuous
nonstop rapids caused by boulders dumped down into the
river when the highway was built. It wasn't a natural set of
rapids—it was just solid rapids. Every individual drop was
just at the limits of what I could handle; when you packed
them all together continuously with no eddies, it was like
packing twenty miles of whitewater into seven miles of
river."

Barrow made it through the first eight or ten moves all
right; then a big wave turned him around, and he started
going backwards down the river. A big hole swallowed him
up and spat him out, and on he went:

"But at that level—whooo!—if I'd been with other people,
hemming and hawing and hand-wringing, I never would

have done it; my perspective gets out of joint about what's reasonable and doable . . .

"The continuity and intensity of it—you get into a different mental state because you have to. There's no moment of stopping and contemplating about what you're going to do. It's like someone pulled the chain, and *boom*, you're gone. Your body kind of takes over—your automatic nervous system, or something; whatever responses you've got from years of paddling. There's a total absence of fear, whereas if you sat around and thought about it, you'd be terrified. You don't think about it because you can't, there's no time."

Some interesting things emerged from these and other accounts of adventure and extreme sport. For one thing, the stress-triggered magic was a hit-and-miss affair, mostly miss. Ninety-nine point nine percent of the time, the games, no matter how desperately bloody they were, did not ignite vision, ecstasy, or supernatural power. The norm was represented by accounts like *The Worst Journey in the World*, the marvelously named Apsley Cherry-Garrard's narrative of Scott's ill-fated British South Pole expedition of 1910–13. Scott and company pushed themselves past threshold after threshold of fatigue, pain, cold, and hunger, and found nothing but misery, madness, and death. Excerpts from the expedition members' journals form a litany of doom: "It is all too horrible. . . . I am almost afraid to go to sleep now." "Evans had such cold hands we camped for lunch . . . The wind is blowing hard, T-21, and there is that curious damp, cold feeling in the air which chills one to the bone in no time. . . . Great God! this is an awful place . . ." "All our feet are getting bad—Wilson's best, my right foot worse, left all right. . . . Amputation is the least I can hope for now." Cherry-Garrard survived the expedition to write his book, culminating in this bitter and eloquent benediction:

And I tell you, if you have the desire for knowledge and power to give it physical expression, go out and explore. If you are a brave man you will do nothing; if you are fearful you may do much, for none but cowards have need to prove their bravery. Some will tell you that you are mad, and nearly all will say: "What is the use?" For we are a nation of shopkeepers, and no shopkeeper will look at research that does not promise him a financial return within a year. And so you will sledge nearly alone, but those with whom you sledge will not be shopkeepers: that is worth a good deal. If you march your Winter Journeys you will have your reward, as long as all you want is a penguin's egg.

I perceived another interesting fact: when stress did produce altered, superior states of consciousness, they seemed to come in two distinct kinds. One, the type exemplified by my experience on Neva and John Muir's on Mount Ritter, consisted of an acrobatic variation on Zen satori: a feeling of mystical interdependence with the outside world, welling up from somewhere deep inside, and manifesting itself physically as acute sensory awareness and a relaxed and boundless strength. The other—Lindbergh's cockpit angels and the Grand Canyon phantoms of Anonymous are perfect examples—took the form of hallucinatory helpers, the athlete or adventurer receiving a transfusion of energy, encouragement, and instinctual wisdom from a seemingly external source—angels, spirit people, whatever. Why the different mode of revelation? Perhaps during times when one is beset by intense loneliness as well as exhaustion, danger, or cold, the illusion of a companion is so necessary that the brain manufactures one for itself.*

The factors that went into causing these athletic satoris were obvious: loneliness, exhaustion, risk, hunger and thirst (often), tied together and intensified by an almost fanatical striving toward a goal: a summit, a river run, a thermal ride to fifteen thousand feet . . . and sometimes, as in my own case, pure survival. But why did the magical response come one time and not, under precisely the same circumstances, the next hundred or thousand or ten thousand times? Until I figured that one out, what happened to me on Mount Neva and how to make it happen again would remain an enigma.

---

* Many Himalayan climbers and Arctic and desert explorers have experienced this mysterious "phantom companion" phenomenon. Eliot referred to it in *The Waste Land:*

> Who is the third who walks always beside you?
> . . . when I look ahead up the white road
> There is always another one walking beside you . . .

3

Meanwhile, I kept on with my own physical, visceral search in the games I played, almost always alone, in the mountain fastnesses west of Boulder. If I didn't quite find what I was looking for, it dead sure wasn't for lack of trying.

Looking back on it now, I think I was subconsciously trying to reduplicate my Neva experience, perhaps naively, perhaps not, by going through the same set of moves that had led up to it. If I had gone up into the mountains alone and climbed my way up an obscure mountain into a beatific state, well, couldn't I do it again?

Of course there is a very old Chinese allegory dealing with that same syndrome, but I hadn't read it back then; and even if I had, there was no guarantee I would have applied it to my own case. In the story, this Fool, the same Fool you find in all myths, carnivals, and jokes, goes out into the woods hunting with his bow and arrow. He hides behind a tree, and after a while a rabbit comes hopping along. Before he can do anything, the hare takes a misguided leap, hits a tree head-on, and knocks himself dead. The Fool, rejoicing, takes the rabbit home, cooks it, and eats it. From that day forth he never takes his bow and arrow when he goes hunting; just goes out into the forest, hides behind a tree, and waits for another rabbit to come along and commit hara-kiri in front of him. In time, of course, he starves to death.

That was me, I guess; but in the meantime there were the mountains, those scores, hundreds of days alone up there. "The high country is heaven," Gary Snyder has written, and he is correct. It was all one great Valhalla to me, from Wild Basin south to St. Mary's Glacier, Nederland to the Hellhole, and all that tumultuous, incandescent landscape in between: the secret passageway of Pawnee Pass; Navajo Peak's crooked canine set in the long jawbone of Niwot Ridge; Isabelle Glacier (who is Isabelle? what is she? a hillock of pearl in the black chasms); the string of polished platinum lakes under the cold shoulder of Storm Peak; the wonderfully named High Lonesome Trail, which ran under the western rim of the Divide, through meadows of flowers and grasses . . . The very rocks and trees up there looked like they had swallowed fire. *Istigkeit* Country: *Istigkeit* is a German word meaning the unadorned essence of things, their Suchness, if you will.

I park my van at road's end, shoulder my pack, and head up the trail. The sun streams down through the roof of the pines, kicking up a music of glints on the dark forest floor. The air is still cold, stinging my legs and hands; it is October, laces of ice at the wrists of the creeks, the aspens rattling their mandarin leaves; the creek-bottom brush is amber, sweet-smelling as applejack. I feel a heightened awareness of things, as I always do when I set out on these mountain trips; it is as if I am stalking something up there, with the absolute intensity of a Stone Age hunter. Well, in a way I am. Another expedition in search of that hidden self, which continues to elude me with maddening ease. No matter what peak I climb, what pass I cross, I am always heading in the same direction—or trying to, anyway.

The trail skirts the right side of a tarn, a mile's worth; past the far end, it crisscrosses a narrow brook, with deep holes where the trout flash like tiny neon signs. Heaves itself up a steep turf hillside, up into meadows where the trees thin out. The world is warming: I take off my sweater, the navy one with the thin red racing stripe, tie it around my waist, and slog on up the valley in turtleneck and shorts. A series of waterfalls bashes down through glassy granite boulders, with a white roar that devours all other sounds. The trees are wind-twisted dwarves here, a gnome corps de ballet, gesticulating from ice-scoured ledges and umber turf.

Another lake, long and thin as a snake and pure ice water. Clear as air; no, clearer: the stones and mud of the bottom are like objects seen through a lens, their edges insistent, snipped out of hollow light. From the opposite ridge, great rockslides descend to the very edge of the lake. On a tiny island of sod, someone has set up a tent of international orange nylon. I look, but I can't see anyone; they must be asleep, or up on the ridges. There are many fine climbs up there, farther to the west, along the Divide.

The trail forks, midway around the right-hand shore. The left-hand trail leads to another tarn, then another, and a hanging glacier in a cul-de-sac of peaks. One of the last glaciers in the Colorado Rockies, this one is shrinking year by year: now a sheet of fossil ice and dusty snow the approximate size of a football field, almost flat at its lower end and near vertical at the top, perhaps a hundred feet thick at

the center . . . Someday it will be no bigger than a doormat:
a glaciologist will come, put it in a suitcase, and take it down
to the university to study it; then it will be filed away in a
black plastic bag in a dark, refrigerated room along with
thirty or forty other glaciers. In the winter the jade icy lumps
will whisper to each other of the Ice Age, when they pushed
rocks the size of office buildings and chased men and
mastodons across the land.

I take the right fork, up the steep sidewall of the valley.
The air is getting skinny, at 10,000 plus feet, and I take my
time. No trees at all now. The path weaves between boulders,
over tundra, a carpet of mosses, tiny leaves, and tinier flowers.
A marmot barks from the screes over to the right; I see a
brown head, like a miniature bear's, gazing at me. Koch, a
ski-bum friend of mine starving in Aspen one summer, tried
hunting marmots for the table. He evolved the following
recipe: "Shoot *Marmota flaviventris* with .22. Put in plastic
garbage bag in backpack, carry back down to road. Drive
home. Skin, clean, chop into stew-sized chunks, cook in water
with carrots, onions, potatoes, A-1 Sauce, salt, pepper, bay
leaf. Simmer all day. Invite woman over for dinner. When
asks what awful smell is, tell her 'Marmot stew.' Allow her to
buy you dinner at Red Onion."

I know these mountains so well by now; they are being
embossed on my heart season by season. There, in that
niche of meadow below, I camped with my wife three years
ago; springtime, masses of wildflowers, a fine rain . . . And
there, in the higher valley, I turned an ankle in the glacial
moraines coming down from a climb and limped eight
miles back to the road, using my ice ax as a crutch, while
Tom Quinn made bad jokes to keep my spirits up: "Some
people will do anything to try and get sympathy." And

there, on a snowfield on the opposite ridge, Bill Day, Muffy
Brewer, and I skied one hot summer's day, carving slushy
turns in the dank, granular junk; we drank Teton Tea
(lemonade, black tea, and white wine), and skied till sunset;
hiked down in the gathering dusk, carrying our skis.

I stop to eat, Bacon Bar and one of the weird orange-
flavored glucose slabs called Turblokken washed down with
snow water. After a few minutes' rest sprawled on the
tundra, I start up the big snowfield below the summit of
the pass. The snow is steep, three hundred vertical feet
from top to bottom, and hard as rock: I wish I had brought
my ice ax and crampons, but no such luck. There are old
tracks, stamped four or five inches into the snowpack and
refrozen; I use them as footholds, moving gingerly from one
to the next: one slip, and it will be a quick and nasty journey
to the rocks below. I fear ice, snow hard as ice, don't like it
at all. It doesn't forgive the slightest mistake. After a couple
of hundred feet the angle eases, and it isn't so bad. Well, by
this afternoon, when I descend, the snow should have mel-
lowed in the sun, enough to make it easier.

The top of the pass: cloud shadows drift over a sea of
broken rock, clumps of dry grass, a Forest Service sign by
the faint trail:

——— Pass
Continental Divide
Altitude 12,180 feet

The other side—I have never gone there, keep meaning to,
but it is a long way—is a mass of cliffs, teetering blocks:
sneeze, and it looks like the whole thing will cut loose. The

trail, etched precariously in the crumbling slopes, leads down to a brilliant turquoise tarn cupped in a granite hand; below, sunlit timber stretches away to more ranges of crumpled stone the color of tin, swatches of dirty snow, the Void.

I climb the peak to the right, the east—no name, just an altitude, 12,900 and some feet—twenty minutes, up the ridge. It smells like rain; farther east, down toward the Great Plains, thunderheads swell. I pull the plastic tube containing the climbers' register out of the summit cairn and sign: the third time I have climbed up here. There are other names I know here: my wife's and Quinn's big, arrogant signature and more . . . Every two or three years the Mountain Club people come up here and put in a new register. What do they do with the old ones? Stashed with the stolen glaciers, I think, in those same campus cellars; dusty reams of them recording climbs from the twenties and thirties, immigrant climbers in knickers and floppy cloth workingman's caps; the forties, 10th Mountain Division troops on leave, Eisenhower jackets and gigantic high-topped boots, rappelling off the cliffs with hemp ropes, smoking cigars, and drinking whiskey from pint flasks . . . If you went back far enough, Arapaho or Ute medicine men looking for visions and eagle feathers (the first white men to climb Long's Peak found an Indian eagle trap at the summit). Every mountaintop has its ghosts.

Sitting there on the ancient granite slabs, my back against the cairn, looking out over the infinite ranges, all inputs are golden; I am at the heart of a perfect orb. Something rings in my ears, mingled with the great, drowsy silence: the music of the spheres? "I heard nothing except the music that had seemed to accompany me throughout my climb," Reinhold

Messner wrote after his solo ascent of Everest in 1979. "It was a very rhythmic music, baroque music. I have tried to recapture the melody since, but it was impossible, the theme has gone forever."

I have heard that music, too, and then lost it when I came down to the "real" world, the flatlands. (It has something to do with the magic I found on Neva; what, I am not sure. Perhaps the tune leads to the magic there, like an unraveling rope.) I keep thinking I can recall it, from the back rooms of my mind, but it just won't come . . . pentatonal, I think, I'm almost sure, like that chant of the monks in Auden, Isherwood, and Britten's quasi-opera *The Ascent of F6*:

> Go ga, morum tonga tara
> Mi no tang hum valka vara
> So so so kum mooni lara . . .

There was a sacred crystal at the monastery on F6: anyone who looked into it saw his or her secret dreams come to life, terrible and beautiful.

Moses went up on Mount Sinai to converse with the deity, and later to receive the Ten Commandments; Mohammed saw visions in a cave on Mount Hira, and Jesus, from what the Gospels tell us, spent many of his most profound times on the desert peaks of the Levant. Sakyamuni Buddha, who was born less than one hundred and fifty miles from the main range of the Himalayas, unaccountably chose to seek Nirvana in the steaming, sunken jungles of the Ganges, but subsequent great followers of the Dharma include several notable mountain men, including Han Shan, the Chinese high-altitude hermit-poet of the T'ien T'ai range, and

Milarepa, the singing saint of Tibet, who composed most of his "Hundred Thousand Songs" far beyond timberline, in the ice caves and gravel deserts of what he called "No Man's Land."

There is something about high places; something about lonely, wild places in general—desert, sea, barren ground, great salt lake—but something in particular about high ones. Some say it is the rarefied air, but I think not: even comparatively low summits (Nowah'wus, Sacred Mountain of the Cheyenne Indians, is a mere 6,000-footer; Mount Sinai's summit is only 8,664 feet above sea level) seem to have the Power. No, there is some other factor involved; perhaps the very physical, metaphysical fact that solid matter, terra firma, comes to a final, pointed end at the summits of peaks, and beyond is the thin realm of blue gases and black space, aether. Until the mid-nineteenth century, when the first balloonists appeared in France, the sky was absolutely off-limits to man: gods and goddesses only. (Recall what happened to Icarus.) Recognizing this, and the magic that kindled at the interface between the two worlds, the ancient Mesopotamians, Egyptians, Chinese, and Mesoamericans all built themselves artificial mountains, pyramids, or ziggurats, reaching off their flat, riverine valley empires to plug into the firmament.

I can feel what they were after here on this sun-consumed rockpile. Eternity is trying to speak—no, sing to me; I can't quite get the message, but it is there. Perhaps, I tell myself, I need to spend longer up here to get it. Come up here with tent, sleeping bag, stove, sack of freeze-dried food, and wait for the music to come. A week, ten days, perhaps a month, in the winter, when nobody is around . . . Let the silence and the emptiness work away at me, abrade away the false self of town and classroom, until I am ready to hear.

After a while I start back down; not the usual route, the way I came up, but east, the Other Side: over a heap of blocks, down into the screes that descend, I see, at least four or five hundred vertical feet to the saddle that leads to the next peak, another nameless one. *No one* ever goes down here, down these chutes of granite garbage. The angle is maybe 35 or 40 degrees, a little more in places: the rock is loose, rotten, too, adding to the difficulty. A piece as big as an *Oxford English Dictionary* squirts from under my boot, sails away into space. It clatters far below, and the sound echoes queasily in my gut. A lot of space down there, as much as I want and maybe a bit more. This is why I came here.

I move with extreme care, totally focused on my hands and feet, and the few square inches of ground under them. There is a kind of meditation the Theravada Buddhists call *vipassana*, the Tibetans *shi-ne*: "single-pointed concentration." It involves meditating on something, anything— pebble, stick, Buddha, syllable, sardine tin—until you are totally consumed by it. Subject, object, the mind-body problem, everything, destroyed, leaving only the act of perceiving. What happened on Neva, of course; and what I hope will happen again here. A gymnastic kind of meditation, paring away the unessential, flensing the moment down to a brilliant core. Fingertips flexed around the flanks of a wobbly boulder, feet splayed on a broken pitch of cliff . . . the left hand sneaks down to a bit of ledge, followed by the right; my left foot searches out a crack between two more rocks: this is all there is.

These are not really hard places by big-time climbing standards, but alone, without a rope for protection, on this lorn mountainside, I find them challenging enough.

These games will be the death of me yet; the wrack and ruin, or else the salvation. Like the *bone games* the Indians of the American West play, where you hide the striped and unmarked bones, one in either fist, and the opponent tries to guess which hand holds which . . . When the magic is really on a roll, when the singing summons up the Power, one can guess right or wrong forty or fifty times running, depending on which end of the Power you are on. You can win the ranch, the Cadillac, a thousand head of prime Black Angus, or lose everything you own—property, love, the works—and go down the road with empty pockets and an empty heart.

These other bone games, of course—climbing, running, trekking, and the rest—are a hundred times more serious: if you lose out here, there won't even be a road to go down, and nobody to go down it anyway. If you win, the whole planet won't hold the ranch you carry away in your empty hands. Games pared down to the blazing bare bones, to the beautiful, terrible core of it all. Nothing left but the player alone playing in and on thin air:

> When you get to the top of the
> mountain, keep climbing,

as the Zen parable says.

I keep on hoping to crack into a moment of transcendence; keep climbing these lonely mountains, but it's not the kind of thing you can really plan for. You put yourself out on the

Edge, and sometimes you get mugged by the angels, sometimes not. But what else can you do?

It strikes me again today, as it almost always does on these hikes and climbs, that I am just not sticking myself far enough out on the edge of things, as far out as I was on Neva. But how can I? I can't go around the Rocky Mountains flinging myself over precipices and hoping I land on tiny ledges, and then hoping that some kind of magic clicks into gear, enough to get me down safely. Even if the superficial dynamics were the same, I am not sure it would work. Perhaps the accidental nature of the event on Neva, the fact that my control over my fate had been wrenched completely from my grasp, against my will, in the instant of falling, had been the real key to what followed. Perhaps the powerful hidden self only appeared when the normal limited self was shocked or scarified or otherwise blown out of the way for an instant, clearing the boards. If so, it would be a pretty hard thing to plan for.

Down through a band of cliffs, the rock unstable as crystal nitro . . . Clouds race overhead, driven on the wind, headlong over the ridgelines like a dream of white horses. I had intended to climb the next peak to the east, traverse over its summit to the 13,900-foot giant to the east, the peak I call Storm, in honor of the heavy weather that brews there. Over Storm's peak, down the southern screes, and back down through the forests to the road. Well, it isn't going to happen. Something big is happening up in the sky, I can smell it. The temperature is skidding down. What time is it? Must be two-thirty at least. I think of a hundred mountaineering accidents I have read about: "As well as events can be reconstructed, the dead man traversed the peak around noon, ignoring the storm that was building up. He descended the saddle to the east, and continued on in worsening conditions. His body, clad in shorts, turtleneck, and climbing boots, was found at the base of a fifty-foot chimney ... Death due to injuries suffered in the fall, and exposure."

It is dark, sunless, now; and from out of the darkness snow begins to fall. It must have been seventy-five or eighty when I started up the pass this morning, not a cloud in the sky; now suddenly it looks like January. The white stuff drizzles down. Thunder cracks over Storm Peak.

These Colorado Rockies have some of the flakiest weather on the planet. The greatest twenty-four-hour snowfall on record occurred not far from here in *April* 1921: 76 inches, nearly 6½ feet. Springtime in the Rockies. I have been bowled over, blown flat on my face, by the chinook winds in the foothills: gusts up over 120 miles an hour, the air full of stones, chimneys, tree limbs. There are Fourth of July blizzards along the Divide, and thunderstorms in the summer that wash out the dirt roads in the gorges.

I bushwhack, or stonewhack, rather, down the screes. Keep losing my way, in the trackless rocks, and finding it again. My USGS map is no good: not enough detail to show the confusion of cliffs, crags, chutes, patches of ice the size of racquetball courts that I creep over carefully, like some celestial cat burglar. Tricky territory, especially with the snow falling and daylight beginning to wane. Again I recall the climbing fatalities I have read about: how many of them began just this way, with slightly awry equipment and clothing (shorts, no ice ax), dodgy weather, unknown terrain ... I force myself to take my time, go slow, suss out my next move before I start it.

By the time I make it down into the uppermost forests, the ground is beginning to whiten; still the stuff sifts down,

tons of it every few seconds, and no end in sight. Up on
the Divide, where I was just three—was it three?—hours
ago, it must be socked in solid: foot-deep drifts in the lee of
the boulders, the trails filling up, the avalanche chutes
cocking their triggers.

My bare legs are numb, the color of modeling clay. Breath
plumes, incandescent. It is getting colder still, and darker.
I hurry now, down through the forests, skidding on the wet
needles. To the road, the car.

The worst thing about old VW vans, besides their incredible gutlessness on steep grades, is their heater system. A
thin pipe carries warm air all the way from the engine com-
partment in the rear, the length of the chassis, and spews
it out under the dashboard; by the time it gets that far, of
course, it is stone cold. I wrap my beloved Mexican blanket,
purchased in the streets of Durango for $12 on a long-ago
surfing trip, around my legs as I drive down the wet, opal
road. The edges of the blacktop are already white; the pines
are silver spikes in the incandescent gloom.

The snow turns to sleet and freezing rain around Ward.
I turn down onto the dirt road to the Plains, Boulder. The
mountains smell sweet and wild, an incense compounded
of wet stone, wet amber brush, wet moss, humus, genera-
tions of pine needles . . . an almost unbearably lovely smell;
despite the cold I pull the window open to catch it all. The
rain hisses down into the black heart of a great mystery that
I am on the very edge of discovering. Any moment now, I
am sure, it will drift in on the mountain rain, into my life.
Only it never ever quite arrives.

That's how it was back then. Life in the mountains, of
the mountains. I was a high-country madman, what the

Japanese call a *yamabushi,* a possessed mountain man, totally hooked on the ranges.

We lived in a cabin up under the Flatirons, those tilted slabs of Fountain Formation sandstone at the southwest edge of Boulder. The trails began a quarter mile up the road, but the wilderness was even closer than that: raccoons and skunks came down every couple of nights to raid the garbage cans—once I watched a huge coon and just as giant a skunk, working together as a team, rock our can back and forth till it tipped over! Deer came down in the winter, herds of two dozen or more, to graze on the lawns.

On the map, that stretch of foothills I roamed was less than fifteen square miles of nothing special: the highest summits were less than 9,000 feet above sea level, the mesas and canyons the usual topography you find along the Rockies' eastern flanks. But to me, somehow, they were a holy land; every time I went up there, a kind of magic happened to me: I felt a nameless wildness flow into me, a strangely serene longing for tundras, unbroken forests, rivers and mountains without end . . . I changed, in a benign kind of lycanthropy.

Green Mountain was my Kailas, Bear Peak my Sinai. There were so many marvelous little niches up there, tiny realms of desert, rain shadow, transition zone, if you looked closely. The southernmost stand of paper birch in America, a dozen trees, their nearest brothers three hundred miles away in the Black Hills of South Dakota. Once, unbelievably, redwood forests covered the area; there were still relict plants from that florid time, waxflowers and Oregon grape. Drizzling microclimates sprouted carrion flower, sarsaparilla, wood lily, rattlesnake fern, bird's-foot violet, lady's slipper, orchids.

I roamed up there endlessly without any thought of time: sometimes I went up into the hills at three in the afternoon, after my last class, and didn't come down till long after dark, nine, nine-thirty at night, stumbling and bumping into trees. Most often alone. Shinnying up those dank dihedrals in the cloudbanks, slogging those trails to where, indeed, Something lurked.

So what was the problem? The same: I was getting 99 percent of the way there ("there" being what had happened to me on Mount Neva), but the last, vital 1 percent that catalyzed it all was still as distant and inaccessible as ever. At least that was how I felt. It was as if there were a membrane clear as air and thinner than the thousandth skin of an onion, a membrane that stretched and stretched but never broke, separating me from what I sought.

A couple of times I blundered accidentally into a situation incredibly similar to the one of Neva: even then the magic didn't click. Once a falling rock nearly brained me during a climb in the crags just west of Boulder . . . but I'll deal with that one later; it has other significances, resonances. Then there was the time I got lost on a traverse of a remote pass, more bad weather, ice on the stones and the steep alpine meadows under skins of crystal; fell a dozen times, banged my wrist badly, took ten wrong turns, and hiked out at dusk, freezing, through an empty valley, across a deserted mesatop. Broke through more second winds than a cat has lives, and then had to negotiate a scarifying iced-up traverse down a 400-foot bluff to the highway in the dark. I got some of the physical effects I had found on Neva—my legs walked on, on pure automatic pilot, long after I had given up on them, and the benighted descent to the road was plain ridiculous—but it was *not the same*. None of the ecstatic feeling of sureness, of being fitted in perfectly to what had formerly been a foreign, disjointed world—no revelation, no satori. Nothing, in short, you could found a religion on.

It reminded me, in a ludicrous way, of a certain friend of mine who was trying to teach himself to levitate. He had convinced himself, in the Great American Fool tradition, that sheer effort was the secret. He used to sit cross-legged in his basement room, for hours, teetering on the clenched cusp of his gluteus maximus, sweat pouring off his brow; if faith could move mountains, he would have shot through the ceiling, out of the house, and into orbit, but it never quite happened. *"I just can't get that last little bit off the ground!"* he would cry out in rage and frustration as another session ended in failure.

Indeed: neither could I. I was close, during those solo mountain games, but no cosmic cigar.

They say that leopards, those cleverest of the great cats, make the same ridiculous mistake over and over and over again: they camouflage themselves perfectly, melding their mottled colors into sunlight and shade, folding their long limbs into the curves of earth, tree, rock . . . The only thing is, they forget to hide their tails: they crouch in ambush, concealed except for that fat, luminous fifth limb wagging back and forth like a flashing electric sign—LEOPARD LEOPARD LEOPARD—and the hunters shoot them like tin cans on a fencepost.

I was making some mistake as horribly simple as that, I thought; some tiny error of the flesh or mind or spirit.

It wasn't going to be enough just bashing away at those games. I would have to apply some thought to it, to try and make things work out right: figure out exactly what was going on out there, and how to do it differently. What I needed, in short, was something like a technical manual for the human mind and body, high-performance situations included; but of course no one had ever written one.

A strange, strange series of incidents kept me going, even when it seemed my quest was dead-ended forever; a promise that there were magical connections to be made out there in the wilds, in those wild games.

I was rock-climbing in California, in the desert west of the Salton Sea, when I came upon a cave high in a cliff. Two owls flew out as I approached from below. I entered the cave and found a huge head-high nest with scores of tiny defecated skeletons of mice littering the rock floor in front of it. I felt like an intruder, and out of shame for having disturbed this sanctum sanctorum, I took out a piece of obsidian I had found a week before beside a sacred lake in the Nevada desert and left it before the nest as a kind of offering.

Some kind of mystical bargain must have been struck there without my knowing it, because for the next year or so I seemed to be guarded, watched over, by owls. I would be walking up a canyon in broad daylight, turn a corner on the trail, and find a great horned owl, big as a bobcat, staring at me from a dead tree not twenty feet away. Camped by a lake in Nevada, I walked out into the dark to answer the call of nature, heard a rustling over my head, raised my flashlight beam, and there were a half-dozen barn owls the color of ghosts, with those flat poker faces, circling overhead. One morning in a wintry canyon in Utah, depressed and out of sorts, I wished for a sign, some kind of a sign, that things would be all right; not five minutes later a shadow grazed my occiput and fled up the cliff face, dropping a single, great barred feather at my feet, not six inches from my shoe.

There *was* a power out there, impossible to explain away or intellectualize, but there it was. I don't know what, if anything, it had to do with my experience on Neva, but it was one more sign that the world was far, far deeper and wider than most of us ever knew. I would have been a fool to turn my back on it.

4

The next step in my search came, strangely enough, from my academic studies in anthropology. I was majoring in the subject at the University of Colorado, with a specialization in Native American and Central Asian shamanism. The more I read about shamanistic ordeals and initiations, the more incredible the parallels between them and the extreme sports I was interested in seemed to be: in fact many of the shamanistic training rituals were really nothing more than extreme games, like mountaineering, distance running, trekking, engineered to deliberately induce the kind of power and ecstasy I had accidentally stumbled upon on Mount Neva.

In August 1979, British climbers on Mount Kenya encountered a lone African man not far from the peak's summit. The man was shoeless, with only wool socks on his feet; he carried a sack of food, twenty-five feet of rope, a bread knife, and a Bible. For the past five days he had been living in a scrap-iron lean-to on top of the mountain; God, he said, had sent him there to pray for the well-being of the world. Now he was on his way down.

The authoritative guidebook *Mountains of the World* describes Mount Kenya this way: "the final 2,000 feet leap upward in tremendous precipices. . . . There is no non-technical route up Mount Kenya, and even the easiest route involves rather difficult rock and ice climbing." It seemed impossible that a lone mystic without boots, crampons, or ice ax could have climbed it. And it seemed even more impossible that he could climb *down* the mountain safely: descending is much more difficult than ascending, without a rope and hardware to rappel off of. The British climbers looked for him during their descent, but there was no sign of him anywhere; they reported him missing, and search parties were sent up onto the peak, but to no avail.

Several days later, when they got to the mountain's base, long after he had been given up for dead, the mystery climber showed up safely at a village at the base of the mountain, and told his story. His name was Ephraim M'Ikiara; he was fifty-two years old, a devout believer in both Christianity and native Kikuyu animism. This was his third ascent of Mount Kenya.

His climbing techniques, as he described them, were fantastical. He hacked holds in the ice and snow with his bread knife and used his food bag, tied to the far end of a rope, as a grappling hook, throwing it up over protuberances on the mountainside and clambering up after it. Without boots or shoes, his feet could cling more easily to the tiniest, most tenuous of rugosities. He also carried the valve assembly of a camp stove; there were abandoned fuel cylinders in the huts on the peak's lower slopes, still containing residues of gas, and all M'Ikiara had to do was plug his valve into them, light up, and cook.

In the Himalayas, the high-altitude zone has long been used by spiritual seekers: Buddhist lamas, Hindu *saddhus,* the shamans called *jangkris* and *dhames*—all go up into the snows to look for power. The 1960 British-New Zealand expedition to 22,494-foot Ama Dablam, just south of Everest, ran into a Nepali hill shaman high on the glacier ice. The Western mountaineers were equipped with down clothing, double-layer boots, sleeping bags and tents, even a prefab metal hut. The shaman wore a pair of slacks, a shirt, and a three-button suit jacket, with nothing on his feet. After one particularly severe blizzard, expedition climbers found him lying on his back on the glacier, dusted with snow, fast asleep. The shaman told the climbers he went up into the high Himal every year to renew his spiritual energy: shades of M'Ikiara.

The tradition of going up into the mountains for power is very, very old in Asia. Milarepa, the ninth-century Tibetan mystic and poet, spent years in the ranges along the Tibetan-Nepalese border, the highest mountains on earth, equipped with only a thin cotton sheet and a bowl. According to Tibetan Buddhist histories, he lived on nettle soup and *tsampa* (roasted barley flour), and practiced a kind of yoga called *tummo* to keep warm: tummo adepts can supposedly generate enough body heat to dry out a waterlogged blanket simply by laying it next to their skin for a few minutes. Can they really? I would not be surprised. In Japan, the yama-bushis practiced Shinto rites and austerities in the high country of Honshu and Hokkaido. The ancient Buddhist and Taoist sages of China's T'ien T'ai range used the high wilderness to hone themselves physically and spiritually.

Most famous of the lot was Han Shan, whose name means "cold mountain" and who lived on a peak by that same name in the T'ien T'ai around a thousand years ago, climbing, meditating and writing poems, also collectively titled *Cold Mountain*. "He looked like a tramp," Chinese official Lü-ch'iu Yin, who visited him, wrote. "His body and face were old and beat. Yet in every word he breathed there was a meaning in line with the subtle principle of things, if you only thought about it deeply." When the pious Lü-ch'iu tried to press gifts on Mister Cold Mountain, the hermit and his monk friend Shih-Te ran away, up into the mountains, and were never seen again. The Cold Mountain Poems, by which we know Han Shan and his Zennish mountaineering career, were copied off the logs and boulders where the poet had carved them.

> Men ask the way to Cold Mountain
> Cold Mountain: there's no through trail . . .

Indeed. Incidentally, these sages were fine climbers. During the Cultural Revolution the Red Guards swarmed up into the T'ien T'ai to destroy the inscriptions these lone holy men left on the cliffs; they had to use elaborate rappel systems, even cables and winches, to reach them.

First, a brief note on nomenclature. From here on in, I will be referring to traditional techniques in which stress is used to invoke personal power as "shamanistic." Shamans are the earliest of religious specialists, going all the way back to the Neolithic, perhaps before, and they were the first to discover the stress-power equation in the human mind and body. Other, later religions ranging from Tantric Buddhism and Hinduism to Judaism and Christianity have drawn from that great old tradition in their own rituals and prayer and meditation techniques, but as shamans really originated the basic ideas, *shamanistic techniques* they shall be called.

Looking at shamanistic traditions around the world, mountain and non-mountain alike, you discover that across the globe shamans, whether you find them in an Arctic Dogrib village or in a rain forest in Laos, share a common list of powers and talents. They are masters of heat and cold, able to withstand inhuman extremes of either. They are supposed to be possessed of phenomenal physical endurance and a supernatural sense of direction. They can juggle and manipulate small objects with amazing dexterity. Their sense of balance is unmatched. They know no fear (more on these last two powers shortly).

There were other talents, of course—healing the sick, predicting weather, and so on—but these were the ones that fascinated me the most; the more I read about them, the more they seemed to have to do with my own experience on Neva. What had happened to me happened to them in their shaman's training, only they held on to the power they found while I lost mine. The list of examples went on and on.

In nineteenth-century Manchuria, the Manchu shamans sought personal strength, or honed powers they already had, by cutting nine holes in the ice of a frozen river, then diving in the first hole, swimming underwater to the second, out to catch breath, back under and on to the third, and so on. The holes were far enough apart that if you missed one, you drowned; tricky business, in the dim and turbulent depths of the river. In another aquatic marathon, a certain modern Rastafarian holy man in Jamaica, member of that fascinating sect that worships Haile Selassie, ganja, and reggae, tests him-

self each year by swimming straight out to sea as far as he
can until he is totally exhausted; then he turns, and tries to
make it back to shore alive. In this way, he replenishes
himself, his strength and nerve.

Among certain Eskimo tribes of Greenland, a young man
who wanted a vision was taken out to a lonely place by a
shaman and left there. For days and nights the acolyte continuously rubbed a small stone on top of a large one until a
spirit appeared, conjured up by the isolation, the monotony,
the lack of sleep. In Australia, Aborigine tribes still use
something called Walkabout to instill strength and wisdom
in their youths. Young men are sent off into the outback
with little more than an atlatl (spear thrower), a water gourd,
and a memorized map of waterholes, game trails, and sacred
tribal places. A youth may wander for weeks, months, sur-
viving on his own, praying at the shrines along the way; he
returns with the image of the tribe's land stamped into his
body and his mind. Some North American Plains Indian
tribes practiced a similar kind of mystery trek: young men
and women wandered solo out across the prairies, looking
for something, Something: for hunger, thirst, fatigue, and
space to ignite a transcendence. The Papago Indians of
southern Arizona and northern Sonora did an arduous forced
march across the volcanic wilderness of the Pinacates Desert
to the Sea of Cortez. There, on the barren beaches, they
gathered salt to carry back to Papagueria, and ran twenty-mile
races on the blazing sand, races whose goal was a life-chang-
ing vision. Some runners ran so hard they died; the fortunate
received visions of white cranes, revolving Magritte mountains, sea spirits, accompanied by magical songs. The vision
and song conferred a power that was supposed to last the
rest of one's life.

Among the Crow of the northern plains, men and women, old and young alike, sought visions. The vision seeker went up into the mountains, alone, where fasting and self-torture were used to break down everyday reality. The anthropologist Robert Lowie described a typical Crow vision quest: "Medicine Crow fasted for four days. He cut off a finger and offered it to the Sun, 'Sun, look at me, I am poor.' . . . The blood poured down. He fell [as if] dead. Toward dawn he saw a young man and young woman coming from the west." These phantoms gave Medicine Crow spiritual instructions, which revitalized his life; he became a ritual leader and a wealthy and powerful man in his tribe.

Certain Indians in Guinea drank great draughts of tobacco juice and wandered alone through the jungles until a vision came. Cochiti Pueblo youths went out into the wilderness for four days and nights without food, praying and singing; spirits came in the form of mountain lions, bears, coyotes, wolves, and eagles. In Nepal, young Sherpa men and women go up onto the mountainsides above their villages, where they meditate for weeks on Tantric Buddhist deities, visualizing the deity's image in the mind's eye, repeating the mantras that invoke the deity's powers. The idea is that something of the god's or goddess's divinity will be transfused into the meditator. Again, sensory deprivation (the meditation is often done in a dark, windowless cell), isolation, and hunger and thirst (meditators are kept on extremely short rations) combine to produce altered states of consciousness.

The Tamang people of Nepal initiate their shamans, called *bombos*, through an elaborate series of stages. First, shaman trainees are taught to drum and sing their way into what the Tamangs call "crazy possession," an uncontrolled god-possessed trance similar to epileptic seizure. In later stages, the trainee learns to control his trances, entering and leaving the trance state at will. In the final initiation, the initiate climbs up into an elevated granary called a *gufa*, a sort of crow's nest on stilts, where he remains for seven days and nights, eating and drinking almost nothing, beating incessantly on his ritual drum, chanting for the gods to come. His guru stays with him the first day and night, giving him instructions and advice; the last six days, the initiate is completely alone, a mystical astronaut in orbit over the ordinary world. When he comes down, he is changed, a different person. He helps run the local community, has the ability in time to lead others along the same visionary path, can heal the sick: a man of parts and powers, in short.

A Cheyenne Indian named William Tall Bull describes a 1947 vision quest he undertook to rid himself of his fear of thunder. He went up into the back hills accompanied by his mother and a shaman named Whistling Elk. After complex ritual preparations involving sage, a buffalo head, a sweat lodge, and the like, Whistling Elk pierced the flesh of Tall Bull's chest with a knife and ran tent pegs through the two sets of wounds; the tent pegs were attached by ropes to a tree, around which Tall Bull then danced, the pegs pulling agonizingly as he leaned his weight back. "It seemed like here was a thing I had to go on with. I couldn't give up."

He smoked a sacred pipe, chanted, and prayed as he danced. A kind of transcendental power seemed to take over, as the night wore on. "I thought of my people, my relatives, the Cheyenne people in general . . . I wasn't in pain. The tiredest part of me was the small of my back." The dancing went on till dawn, when Alex Brady, Whistling Elk's assistant, came and cut Tall Bull loose. "I was just as happy as could be. When you talk of something of such joy, you spoil it . . . I was walking on air . . . I wanted to touch everything." More complicated prayers and sweats followed the ceremony; Tall Bull never panicked at the sound of thunder again, and became, instead of a nervous, unimpressive sort of fellow, a real Cheyenne Mensch.

The Salish Indians of coastal British Columbia and Washington perform a Spirit Dance initiation in which a whole plethora of stresses are used to put candidates into altered states of consciousness, and bring them out the other side stronger, "better." According to anthropologist/psychiatrist Wolfgang Jilek, the unsuspecting initiate is grabbed, bound, and blindfolded, ritually "killed" with a ceremonial club, beaten, bitten, pinched, starved, and deprived of water for four or five days (the ritual masters tease the initiate by holding salmon just out of his reach, or serving him water in impossibly leaky cups!), forced to run through the brush till he collapses, doused with cold water or forced to bathe in icy rivers, hypnotized with nonstop drumming, forced to lie absolutely motionless for four or more days, deprived of sleep, swirled and flung through the air, marched barefoot through snow—enough raw hardship and duress to shock a vision out of practically anyone. This is no aimless sadomasochistic exercise: the initiation culminates in a spontaneous, ecstatic song, and, with it, a sudden blossoming of powers. One modern Salish Spirit Dancer who had lived on the hard side of white men's cities and then returned to the reservation described his peak experience in this rather unusual way:

I was jumping three feet high and I had such a thrill, a terrific feeling as if you were floating, as if you were in the air, you feel really high. I've only had such a feeling once before in my life when I was on heroin mainlining, but then I went through hell afterwards, it was terrible—but with the spirit song's power you get this feeling without the terrible aftermath.

The correlations between what shaman types do and what extreme athletes and adventurers do were obvious: both used risk, exhaustion, and so forth to break through into more intense, potent states of being. What made the former so interesting was that the supposed primitives succeeded where the latter all too often failed.

There are dozens, scores, of accounts in the comparative religious and anthropological literature of shamans finding the stress-triggered power and actually holding on to it, using it. One example: travelers in Central Asia circa 1930 saw spirit oracles in Buddhist monasteries who went through unbelievable transformations when they were put into their trance states. Real Jekyll and Hyde stuff: a small, frail man, for instance, would swell into a black-faced giant who seized high-temper steel swords and twisted them like corkscrews, and had to be restrained by goon squads of lamas. The British Orientalist John Blofeld ran into one such oracle in a Beijing temple in the thirties: "[the oracle] had undergone a remarkable facial change . . . a younger, stronger and more vigorous, *leaner* man had taken his place. . . . I felt absolutely convinced that the figure seated next to me was that of a stranger who had not been there when I entered the room! I cannot remember ever having experienced a sensation of greater horror."

Incidentally, the oracles did not control their own altered states of consciousness and hyped-up physical prowess: Buddhist monk handlers put them in and out of the state by reciting certain mantras. If I may be allowed an irresponsible and impious thought, imagine that Central Asian trance-inducing technology in the hands of a National Football League coaching staff: thudding drums and spectral chanting from the locker room before game time, and then up the ramp surges a mob of staring, foaming, gibbering giants, howling maledictions in liturgical Tibetan and squeezing footballs till they pop like soap bubbles . . .

But back to the idea that shamans and their brethren *are* capable of superhuman exploits. Dr. Andrew Weil, author of *The Natural Mind* and other important works on non-Western medicine and healing, tells of an encounter with a South American medicine man, in the Amazon Basin, who "was the most energetic human being I have ever seen. He would stay up all night, drinking *aguardiente* [alcoholic spirits] and ayahuasca [a violently hallucinogenic decoction made from various tropical plants], chanting, dancing, doing his rituals—very, very strenuous activity. Then, at dawn, he would walk out to his fields and work for hours chopping brush, clearing underbrush—the most back-breaking kind of labor. He never seemed to tire at all. It was quite remarkable."

I saw something of shamanism's potency in Nepal a few years ago on a trek with three other Americans into the remote Hinku Valley east of Mount Everest. We hired about a half-dozen Sherpas and Tibetans to carry our gear.

The third day out, we crossed the 16,000-foot Zatr Og, a nasty snow- and ice-covered pass that led from the Khumbu Valley over into the Hinku. A bad place, snow hard and slick as marble, steep, and plenty of exposure; an American climber had bought it up there the year before.

The descent into the Hinku began down long rockslides, mysterious in the shrouds of mist: then we skirted patches of alpine meadow, abandoned stone huts and shrines. *Goraks,*

the ravens of the Himalaya (named onomatopoetically after
their hoarse song), flapped by in the dimness.

We camped that night in the forests high above the Hinku
River. It began to snow around dusk. We sat out the storm
all the next day and the night after, watching the white
stuff drizzle down through the pine and bamboo, tap its
airy fingernails against the roof of the tent.

The fifth day out of Lukla the sun broke through again;
we followed the west bank of the river north, through
eerie moss-draped forests. Big snow mountains, Mera, Kusum
Kangerru, and others without names, soared to the east, west,
and north. There were wolf droppings on the trail, and
eagles swooped over so low we could hear their pinions
rattle. We saw only one person not of our party, a tiny,
goitered Sherpa man bent like a troll under a wicker basket
pack full of potatoes, heading up toward the pass called
Zatr Og. The Hinku Valley was a wild, wild place. According to some Sherpa myths, it leads to Shambala, the
hidden mountain kingdom that inspired James Hilton's *Lost
Horizon,* Shangri-La. You could believe in the magic there.

The strange things began to happen that evening when
we arrived at our next campsite high up the valley. The sun
was going down; mournful rose light poured between the
mountains, over the boulder-studded tundra that surrounded
us. The clouds were moving in again, bearing the promise
of more snow. We had just pitched our tents and gotten a
fire going when Khancha, our cookboy, staggered into camp
and collapsed on the ground, groaning. Gordon, unofficial
group leader and our most fluent Nepali speaker, asked him
what was wrong, and he replied that there was a hole in his
leg, and his life was draining out of it. How did this happen?
Gordon asked. *A curse,* the cookboy said; *Tenzing put a*

curse on me. He carved it on a piece of wood and hid it in my hat, and recited a mantra at me backwards, and now I am going to die. Khancha lay there on the ground, writhing and shivering like a man in a high fever. Tenzing, a twelve-year-old orphan boy and the youngest of our porters, sat off by himself in the meadows along the river. The other porters muttered amongst themselves; they wanted to beat Tenzing to death, to break the spell.

The story behind all this, as Gordon gradually put it to-gether, was this. Tenzing was an orphan, and a poor one, with no relatives solvent enough to take him in. He was wandering homeless in the jungles south of Phaksumdo when he met, in his words (Gordon translating), "a green man as tall as your hip." The forest *jangkri*—for that, indeed, was what he was—took the orphan in and taught him the secrets of the craft over a period of two years or so.

Tenzing then left his strange master and wandered over into the Solo Khumbu Valley, just below Everest. He was at the big weekly bazaar in the village of Namche when he met Khancha and Khancha's wife; they were looking for an indentured farmhand, and he agreed to sign on with them for a year. It wasn't until they got home, to Khumjung, that the boy let slip that he was a shaman, and a very powerful one. His employers were not pleased at the news—horrified, is more like it—but they kept him on, and the two sides, nervous employers and eerie employee, settled down to an uneasy routine, which took a new turn when the three of them hiked down to Lukla and signed on en masse as porters for our unsuspecting group.

The real trouble had begun at our last campsite before crossing the Zatr Og. The cookboy had gone off to find water, and discovering that the only spring in the area was frozen, had used an ice ax to chop off blocks of ice to melt on the fire. According to the boy shaman, this hammering was offensive to the spirit or *lha* who lived in the spring; when Khancha told him to mind his own business, Tenzing put the curse on him.

After some delicate negotiating by Gordon, Tenzing agreed to remove his curse; in return, the other porters agreed not to harm him. The boy warlock led his victim behind the huge glacial erratic in the center of our camp; a few minutes later we heard him chant, a high-pitched singsong that seemed to come from a long, long ways away; his shadow leaped and strutted in the refracted firelight. Exorcism, Himalayan style. It was as if we had left the twentieth century behind when we stepped over the frozen threshhold of the Zatr Og; we were Somewhere Else now.

The chanting went on far into the night; in the morning the cookboy reported that he was feeling better. By now it was snowing again on the high peaks, threatening to block our return to the Khumbu. We broke camp and retraced our steps toward the pass.

So far the story is a curiosity, nothing more. Psychosomatic curses and cures are common in the anthropological literature. If Tenzing had twisted Khancha's own superstitions back on him and then pulled the trigger on them, so what?

But there was more. On the trip out, we began to notice things about Tenzing, strange things, things that were difficult to deal with in rational terms. Camped, or stopping to rest, we would see him run off, laughing wildly, vanishing in the rocks and trees; a half hour later he would reappear from the opposite direction, smiling a smile that said, *I know something that you don't know. And I know that you know that I know.*

His physical prowess was totally beyond credibility. He would be trudging up the trail, the heavy *doko* (basket pack) on his back, and suddenly without warning he would let it fall and bound up an overhanging cliff face or boulder above the trail. He would hang there twenty feet off the ground, laughing, and then suddenly let go, drop to the ground like a cat, take up his pack, and race on up the trail. His moves were as smooth and fine—no, smoother and finer than those of any professional rock climber or Olympic gymnast I have even seen.

The last day of the trek, we found ourselves on that treacherous west face of Zatr Og again; it was afternoon, and we were hurrying to get back down to Lukla before dark. It had been snowing up there on and off for four days, and the snowfield had several inches of new stuff on it, talcum powder on greased marble: perfect for avalanches, falls, and other bad things. Aleister Crowley, the famous English diabolist, poet, and climber, was driven off Kanchenjunga in the twenties by raging blizzards and drastic snow and ice; a kind of mad panic seized him, and drove him headlong from the mountain, from the Himalayas, never to return: "The Great Fear," Crowley called it later. I caught a taste of that feeling now: doom in the throat, disaster on the tongue, a thousand false premonitions racing up and down my spine like ice mice.

We distributed our ice axes among our porters, who needed them more than we did: they were wearing the usual slick rubber-soled Chinese gym shoes the Nepali hill people hike in, if they have any shoes at all. We descended slowly, gingerly, zigzagging down in single file: the nitro ballet.

Halfway down, Meredith, Gordon's wife, slipped off the track and fell fifteen or twenty feet before she could catch herself. (Meredith is an expert climber and skier, by the way.) She got to her feet in time to see Tenzing *somersaulting* past her down the dread 35-degree snows, his laughter ringing out, golden and unequivocal, in the hard blue air.

All right: given that shamans and similar mystical technicians use what are essentially sports—climbing, trekking, distance running, swimming, whatever—to become superior beings; and given that they seem to succeed much of the time. The next question was obvious: why did the games work for them and not for us?*

The main reason seemed to be that shamanistic initiations are far more complicated than our game-playing: I called them techniques before, and that is what they really are. Comparing our athletic ecstasy-seeking with a Cheyenne vision quest, say, or a Sherpa meditation retreat, is like comparing a glow-in-the-dark Frisbee to an Apple Macintosh or a Lockheed Tristar . . . something like that.

Take, for instance, the initiation of a Caribou Eskimo shaman named Igjugarjuk as recorded by the Danish ethnographer Knut Rasmussen in the 1920s. Igjugarjuk's teacher, Perqanaq, began by putting him through a five-day fast, which ended with a drink of warm water. Another fifteen-

---

* For more accounts of the physical and mental prowess of shaman types, see Lamb's *Wizard of the Upper Amazon,* Halifax's *Shamanic Voices,* and Myerhoff's *Peyote Hunt.*

day fast followed, again ended with a ritual draft of warm
water (the warmth of the water, for reasons we can only
wonder at, was of absolute importance: the gods, according
to Perqanaq, would abandon the initiate if he broke his fast
with cold water). Then a ten-day fast, and then for "five
moons" a diet in which all foods other than lean meat were
strictly proscribed: none of the heart, liver, or entrails that
are such an important part of the regular Caribou Eskimo
diet. For the five moons that followed, Igjugarjuk was
allowed to eat anything he wanted; after that, he went back
onto the lean meat diet of before. Again, it all seems inexplicable, but it is all part of a system, a system we are
seeing only the very outer edge of.

After the hunger, the trial by cold: Perqanaq seated
Igjugarjuk on a sled and dragged him far out into the wilderness at night. It was midwinter. Perqanaq left him out there
in a tiny crude igloo with only a piece of hide to lie on, and
no covering, and, as far as we can tell from the account, no
clothing. Sealed up inside, Igjugarjuk sat in the cold and
dark for five days; on the fifth day, Perqanaq left him a
caribou skin full of water, and departed again.

Igjugarjuk lay there for fifteen days more, living on nothing but water; on the fifteenth day, Perqanaq came again,
again without speaking, and left him another sack of water.
It wasn't till the thirtieth day that a vision came to Igjugarjuk,
of a lovely spirit woman who gave him the power of a
shaman; in return, he belonged to the gods for the rest of
his life.

A kind of trigger mechanism was inserted into the experience by Perqanaq. Throughout the rest of his life, whenever he wanted to invoke his shaman's powers, Igjugarjuk
had to go out into the tundra alone and walk for two or

three days and nights without stopping; only when he collapsed from exhaustion and sleeplessness did the full force rush back into him.

The superficial things that led to Igjugarjuk's vision experience are all very obvious, and complicated enough in and of themselves: the loneliness, the hunger, thirst and cold, all layered in stages, programmed to keep the initiate alive while pushing him to the very edge of death, where magic dwells. But there is much more to it than that, much that we don't really know about: the secret oral instructions given by Perqanaq throughout the long initiation process, the subtle nonverbal cuings, the importance of little things that might seem to us totally irrelevant. Does the warm water, on some mythic level, symbolize the warm blood of a friendly earth, communion with the biosphere? And what of the rank mammal taste of the water from the skin bag? Is that more communion with the biosphere, to further dissolve the boundaries between self and world? Who knows?

Many of the specific details of the initiation process seem insignificant and arbitrary, but I suspect they are not. Who knows what arcane but very real function they have, in the transcendence process? The ignition coil of your Toyota, after all, might not look like anything important to a Stone Age tribesman, but without it, no go.

Drumming, for instance: drumming is traditionally a key part of the shaman's worldwide repertoire; for decades, anthropologists and scholars of comparative religion treated the shaman's drum as an interesting piece of symbolism and an artistic artifact, but nothing else. In recent years, studies by Neher, Jilek, Harner and others have shown that shaman drumming rhythms, at approximately three to eight cycles per second, produce trance states in test subjects. To quote

Jilek: "Due the presence of theta rhythms (4–7 cps) in the electrical activity of the temporal auditory region of the cerebral cortex, experimental subjects react to intensive rhythmic drumming in this frequency range by showing . . . responses in their EEG similar to those described in trance states." Shamans always *said* they drummed people into trances and visions, and now it turns out they do exactly that. A young American anthropologist named Larry Peters found this out in person when he apprenticed himself to a Tamang shaman in Kathmandu, Nepal, during the late 1970s. The shaman, Bhirendra, put Peters into a trance state using a drumming technique different from the one already described: Peters and the other "native" shaman initiates drummed an increasingly louder and more rapid rhythm of double clusters of three beats each—/// ///, /// ///— and when a certain intensity had been reached, Bhirendra inserted a sudden loud beat of his own *between* the beats of his disciples. Peters felt a "tremendous amount of nervous energy" rise through his body, finally centering in his head. His consciousness seemed to leave his body; it flew through the night sky toward a distant greenish glow, which, as Peters approached, turned out to be emanating from a three-story brick building. Through an open window, Peters saw "the upper torso of a green figure . . . the green light emanated from what seemed to be an eye. I realized that I was dreaming, and felt water being poured on my head."

Eventually Peters suffered a kind of delayed culture shock and went back to the States to resume a more prosaic life in the academic world. He tells the story in his obscure but delightful book, *Ecstasy and Healing in Nepal*.

The point is, many, if not most, of the elements in the shamanistic initiation really did work to reprogram the human animal in positive ways; and just as important, many of these same elements can be used, emphasized, in our game-playing, to help assure we find the power we are looking for.

The idea of isolation, loneliness, for instance: shamans used it explicitly to break down the everyday consensual reality most of us never escape. We constantly reinforce a kind of group-hallucination world when we are around other human beings, bending and shaping what we see, hear, and feel with grammar, belief, custom. Solo vision quests and games take us out into a nascent, analphabetic space, a sort of intellectual free-fire zone, where reality is in effect up for grabs, and the possibilities well-nigh endless. When the Dakota medicine man Crazy Horse had his vision of "Many Soldiers Falling into Camp" that enabled him to predict Custer's Little Big Horn attack and ambush it successfully, he was in that zone. Ditto, Blake when he saw the trees full of angels, Mohammed, Moses, and Jesus revelating in the Levantine deserts, Buddha under the Bo-tree, and so forth; there is a potency in solitude that surpasseth understanding. Playing these games solo, noncompetitively, we enter that same marvelous turf; the same games played in groups, as contests, are just not the same.

Another thing: shamans pushed their ritual games and ordeals to the very limits of possibility; if the situation wasn't drastic, the magic wouldn't come. Those power-giving gods loved gamblers; they seldom appeared to anyone but the hardest-core risk takers, the exhausted ones who pushed their way through second, fifth, fiftieth winds till there were none left. You had to play hard to get it: recall Hard Bull pierced through the chest, or Igjugarjuk starving in his chamber of ice.

Also, and trickiest and perhaps most important of all, was the idea of a trigger; this was what made shamanistic and similar initiation techniques so special, so peculiarly sophisticated. Somehow they had figured out a way of recouping that stress-induced power later, at will; summoning up the strength, the spirit, the keenness of sense and mind, whenever it was needed.

Unfortunately, there are no really good, clear descriptions of how the shaman teacher installs the trigger device in his pupil; the drumming accounts are interesting, but they really lie outside the mainstream of stress-based initiation this book is concerned with. Of those cases where power is conferred through carefully programmed stress, in a form that the initiate can retrieve again and again in his later life, we know very little. We know that poor Igjugarjuk, whenever he wanted to get his shaman self revitalized, actually had to go out and give himself a dose of the initiation torment; but there must be more useful, more sophisticated techniques out there waiting to be uncovered. What does the teacher whisper in his pupil's ear at the height of a Plains vision fast to coalesce that precisely right song? What instructions did Medicine Crow receive before his fast and self-mutilation to turn the whole exercise into something more than a gruesome exercise in torture, and to put those phantoms and their lessons into his mind, available to be drawn out by the nearness of death? Songs, mantras, magical formulas, the combination to the mysterious safe inside us all—we still know almost nothing of that. There are great secrets out there still to be learned.

Satori, the Zen experience of the enlightened state, is supposed to be like that, according to the traditional texts. You meditate and meditate and meditate some more, weeks, years of sitting on your haunches on hardwood floors, coccyx howling in anguish, skull splitting with a combination of boredom and baffled rage at some awful riddle—"Who am I?" "What was my face before I was born?"—until perhaps you finally crack through. And when at last you do, it has nothing at all to do with any of the effort you put into getting it: it is an absolutely unconditioned moment, without causes.

Magical performances in games are like that. They too seem to exist on a different plane altogether than the unmagical performances that precede them.

In the two or three months before Neva, I had done scores of climbs on the sandstone slabs and cliffs above Boulder. Sometimes I climbed smoothly and well, other times poorly and awkwardly, but never did any of those earlier climbs partake of the special power I was to find after my fall on that obscure wall. They seemed to be completely different verbs, that "climbing" and that other "Climbing": as unalike as meteorites and potatoes. And yet, thinking about it, they must have had something to do with one another. I couldn't have just gone up on Neva, fallen, and gotten that superhuman state if the skills hadn't already been planted in me, lying there dormant. Somehow I had to learn in order to forget, in order to act: a backwards, but perfect, kind of praxis. You have to walk before you run, and run before you Run. Or as Jack Kerouac once wrote, "Walking on water wasn't built in a day": without limits. It happens almost *in spite of* your meditation. At the same time, if you hadn't meditated, you never would have gotten there at all: one of those delightfully obnoxious paradoxes that lurk beneath the surface of things.

One of those insufferably clever Asian parables that

illustrate delightfully obnoxious paradoxes concerns the frog who falls into a jug of cream; he paddles and scrabbles frantically, trying to stay afloat and get out, but the slippery overhanging walls of the jug defeat him again and again. He is near exhaustion, about to give up, when he discovers that all of his furious activity has curdled the cream into a reef of solidifying butter; a few more moments of clambering, and he is standing on a firm island. He jumps free with the greatest of ease.

5

My next experiment in extreme sport took the form of a long, long trek in the rain, across the rough hill country of eastern Nepal to the base of Mount Everest.

There were precedents, of course: the idea of tramping to spiritual glory did not spring full-blown from my own skull. Zen Buddhists have used walking as a meditation for a long time, pacing back and forth, hands clasped behind their backs, meditating on koans like "Does a dog have Buddha-nature?" or "Why did Bodhidharma come from the West?" In fact, sitting (*zazen*) and walking (*kinhin*) are the very meat, or soy substitute, of Zen. As mentioned before, Plains Indians and Australian Aborigines have rites of passage based on long-distance solo walking. And how much does the institution of pilgrimage, be it Hopis to the sacred Little Colorado salt cave, Hindus to the Ganges, Moslems to Mecca and Al-Medina, or whatever, owe its original importance to the idea of physically *walking* to holiness? A lot, I think: pilgrimage by bus, train, plane, or car is a poor

imitation of the real thing, missing the physical and psychological rigors that give the act its real substance.

I am thinking explicitly of the walking and bowing rituals
of the Tibetan Buddhists, which combine calisthenics and
prayer over courses that may cover dozens, even hundreds
of miles: take a step, pray with hands clasped, down to the
knees, flat on one's belly and face (arms outstretched), and
then up again, another step, inchworming across the landscape. According to High Lamas, the physical act is as much
the key as the faith: breaking down pride, ego and ignorance
with one's own muscles and bones. Some pious Tibetans do
this all the way around Mount Kailas, in western Tibet,
crossing fifteen-thousand-foot passes and such as they go.

There was another, more immediate inspiration for my
Long Walk idea. For the two months before my arrival in
Nepal, I had been studying under a Tibetan Buddhist monk
in northern India. Geshe Ngawang Darjay was his name, a
squat, burly little mountain of a man, brown as a penny and
as wise as you can get: *geshe* means "master" in Tibetan,
and like *roshi* in Zen it denotes someone who has mastered
the painful intricacies of existence in all its categories. He
taught us, me and the other Western pupils at the Tibetan
Library, the rudiments of meditation, a few cycles of mantras, the lessons of faith, skill, and compassion that Buddhism
is founded on. But it wasn't so much what he *taught* as
what he *was* that inspired me. Though he wasn't technically
a shaman, of course—Tibetan Buddhism draws heavily on
ancient shamanistic traditions but is a more sophisticated,
modern faith—he had those same shamanistic attributes that
had interested me so much in my readings. I never saw him
dance on a precipice or bend steel swords into corkscrews,

but he had that same aura of physical and mental certainty,
no false moves and no mistakes. He moved in a state of
perpetual perfection, absolute attention to what was going
on, dealing with everything that came along with a black
belt's quickness and grace. Hard to describe—you really had
to be there to see him—but let me try. Someone once asked
him if Buddha would walk the same way at the brink of a
cliff and across flat ground. "No," he said, "Buddha would
pay attention to the cliff, but he would not be afraid." Someone else asked him what he, the Geshe, would do if he met
a tiger in the forest; I think the questioner expected some
magical answer, but the Geshe laughed and laughed and
said, "Run away as fast as I can!"

I was walking through the cedar woods below town one
day when I saw the Geshe walking along in his robes and
rubber flip-flops, carrying a bundle of Tibetan liturgical
books. He seemed to almost *flow* along the trail, as if he were
on invisible wheels, and he was chuckling to himself as he
went, actually rubbing his hands together in glee. And the
way he *sat,* on his raised platform when he preached the
Dharma: like a block of iron, a boulder, an alp, yet you felt
that if he had wanted to, he could have leapt to his feet in
an instant, like Nijinsky's Faun.

When I left northern India and the Geshe for Nepal, I
had somehow conceived the idea—Geshe Ngawang Darjay
himself would probably have smiled at the naiveté of it if I
had told him about it—that the place to find that wisdom,
or talent, was high up in the Himalayas. The memory of
Neva worked into it too, of course, and also the great Tibetan
tradition of Milarepa, the patron saint of all mountain
mystics, who wrote of the Himalayas:

In the mountains
there is a strange bazaar,
where one may trade the noise and confusion of
    everyday life
for eternal bliss.

And then there was the story making the rounds in
Kathmandu, the capital of Nepal, when I got there. Supposedly some Western climbers had chartered a Pilatius
Porter airplane recently and used it to overfly Lhotse (the
world's second highest peak at 27,923 feet) and photograph
the huge, probably unclimbable back side of the mountain.
The Westerners brought their photos back to Kathmandu and
blew them up, and lo and behold, on one shot, sitting there
in the middle of the Lhotse Wall, a vertical mile up, was a
saddhu, a Hindu yogi, naked except for a big white Saint
Nicholas beard, perched on a ledge no wider than a ballerina's
wrist.

So the story went; and I believed it, too. Why not?

Anyhow, I determined to do it, trek to Everest: a make-
or-break trudge to the dead end of the world. It was the
monsoon season, the time of heavy rains, when the Himalayas
are slick with mud and squirming with bloodthirsty leeches.
Trails wash out, bridges are swept away, and whole villages
plummet into the Void. DON'T GO TREKKING IN MONSOON!
someone had written in the Trek Book at Tashi's Restaurant,
where people inscribed the annals of their mountain hegiras.
I had almost no money, a lingering case of dysentery, maybe
hepatitis, and I spoke about five words of Nepali. Perfect
vision-hunting conditions: "Who dares, wins," as the British
SAS commandos say.

. . .

The bus from Kathmandu to the Chinese border leaves at
7:00 A.M. I wake up late in my dingy 25¢-a-night hotel
room, run to the bus station, and get there at 7:30; the bus
is just pulling out—a giant tin bald-tired monstrosity jammed
to the roof with laughing, chattering Nepalis. I crawl up
into the belly of the monster, and off we go.

I have my trekking permit, from the Chief of Police of
All Nepal, allowing me passage by foot to Mount Everest,
and a weird agglutination of gear, most of it purchased or
bartered in the local bazaars: a canvas German rucksack; a
"Red" Chinese poncho; wool Nepalese army socks; a bundle
of plastic for bivouacs; a two-pound tin of Indian dried milk;
an ancient black-patina Sierra Cup; an equally ancient down
bag; a medical kit—Band-Aids, Lomotil, mexaform, and
Indian one-a-day vitamins of questionable potency; a book of
Tibetan poems in translation; and a locally printed Mandala
Map purporting to show the route to Everest, but with (it
later turns out) villages misplaced by miles, altitudes thousands of feet off, and Everest itself stuck in the wrong massif
altogether!

All this, and the clothes on my back: an Indian T-shirt,
shrunk three sizes the first time it was washed; a khaki Boy
Scout shirt bought in the Kabul, Afghanistan, bazaar; a
Tibetan wool sweater; ragged cutoffs; secondhand kletter
shoes. The whole ensemble is topped by a sporty green-and-
black Tibetan wool hat the size of a bowling ball.

After four hours of drizzling mountain valleys, the bus
drops me off in Lamosangu, jumping-off point for the
Everest trek. I stand in the stone streets, pack on my back.
Filthy little bazaar town. On either side, steep rainy hillsides

rise thousands of feet into the clouds. That famous Kipling line pops into my skull—"A Fool lies here who tried to hustle the East."

Suddenly I feel very, very much alone, and strange, and small. I think of Maurice Wilson, that eccentric British food faddist and mystic who perished alone on Everest in 1933. He had piloted a tiny single-seater airplane from England to India, intending to crash-land it on the summit of Everest; he had a theory that by getting to the top of the world's highest peak alone, he would somehow trigger a spiritual revolution affecting all of mankind. British authorities in India confiscated Wilson's plane, so he continued on up to Sikkim on his own, overland. After lying doggo for a few months to lull the authorities into thinking he had given up, he sneaked across the border into Tibet with a few Sherpa guides and started walking toward the highest mountain in the world. They trekked across the wintry Tibetan Plateau, and after visiting the Rongbuk Monastery at Everest's base, started up the peak. The weather was dreadful; the Sherpas turned back, and Wilson himself was forced to return to Rongbuk, to shelter from the blizzards. After a few days he started up the mountain again, and froze to death alone on the Rongbuk Glacier. His corpse and notebooks were found by members of the 1934 British Everest Expedition, who brought the papers down but left the body; the big Chinese Everest team of the late seventies found the corpse again, and made a ghastly color film of it.

Ah, the pathology of the dreamer; you dream not wisely but too well, and find yourself dancing on black ice in a high, howling Hell, without a leg to stand on. Panic is the other side of the coin of ecstasy, and you lose as often as you win. *What am I doing here, anyway?* I ask myself. I can't think of a good answer, but off I go. Put one foot ahead of the other, and so on, up the trail. Some pilgrim.

Lamosangu lies at 2,500 feet above sea level, in its deep river gorge; the pass I have to cross today, Nigali, is 8,000 plus: five and a half thousand feet to climb, more than a vertical mile.

All afternoon I trudge upward, past terraced farms, through patches of forest, stopping every hour or so at *chai-houses** to get out of the rain and have a cuppa, buffalo milk and sugar making the tea heavy and sweet. The hillsides go on and on interminably. I end up hiking with a little *kuli* (porter) I have met, who is also bound for Nigali, his home village, up on the pass—a tiny, featherweight barefoot hill-man in ragged shorts and a ragged shirt, a huge wicker basket pack on his back supported by a rope around his forehead.

There are dozens of kulis of every caste and tribe imaginable on the trail—Sunwaris, Tamangs, Magars, Jirels, Chetris, Kirantis, Gurungs—many of them women. Tough people: they carry loads of ninety, a hundred, even two hundred pounds on the steep trails day in and day out. Footpaths are the only means of travel and transport over the hills and mountains of Nepal, except for a few roads, and pack animals are rare: almost everything—cigarettes, biscuits, grain, potatoes, butter, kerosene; even firewood, lumber, building stone, and tools—goes on the backs of kulis, who hike all day on a diet of *tsampa* (roasted barley flour) mixed with *chung* (native beer), tea, maybe a potato —more on Kuli Power later.

* Literally, teahouses, usually including a rude sort of café (boiled spuds, rice, tea, biscuits, etc.), a rudimentary general store, and a hostel.

Late in the afternoon, my accidental companion and I climb up to the forbidding ridgeline itself, a stony goblinesque rampart with twisted trees silhouetted against the dark wet sky.

We follow this ridge up as the day darkens and the rain pelts down. The trail is steeper than ever; in places it is an actual stone staircase leading up into the mists. We pass tumbledown shrines, clusters of two-story earthen farmhouses. Fog, drifting clouds. I shiver under my poncho and sweater; my almost-naked fellow traveler trudges on, smiling happily, as if this were a perfect day: perhaps to him all days are perfect. How insufficient I am, think I.

At last, in the evening, we reach the crest, Nigali: a terrace, a chai-house. My kuli friend is home. We say goodbye, in broken English and Nepali—he invites me to stay at his house, a hundred yards or so off the trail, but I am bound, I have already decided, for Shera, another village which the map says is just a mile past Nigali. The kuli smiles and waves one last time; the night swallows him up.

I hike on in the dark: stone walls, forests, empty fields in the rain. The trail switchbacks downward, jumbled with rocks. It's a gloomy scene. Finally, I come to another chai-house; not Shera, no sign of a village, but I decide to stop for the night. I can't see a thing.

Dinner is rice and boiled vegetables, three rupees, and bed on straw-covered boards.

The dawn comes up like nothing, drizzling and dark. I head down toward Shera, through scrub brush.

About an hour out, I meet a kuli who has stopped to pick a leech from between his toes. Hmm, I think: perhaps some of the little devils have gotten on *me*. All the leech horror

stories from Kathmandu trekking lore come back to me: of
trekkers and climbers covered with fat, swollen, blood-oozing
leeches head to toe; of the Giant Green Leeches, long as a
loose bootlace, each capable of sucking a good half pint of
blood out of you. I lean on a rock, take off my boots, peel
down my socks: yes, there are five or six of the rubbery brown
creatures on each foot, mouths embedded in my flesh, rivulets
of blood. I pull them loose and toss them into the brush. The
kuli, watching me, gives a moan of sympathy: "Oooh, sahib."
"It's not that bad," I say foolishly in English. "Only
leeches."

Looking at the ground, I see many more of the hideous
little carnivore worms, inching their way toward me in a
dreadful parody of the movements of prostrating Tibetan
pilgrims, lifting their blind snouts every few seconds to home
in on my body heat: without blood to bloat them, they were
as thin as dental floss. Hurriedly I put socks and boots on
again and start walking; a couple more have already made it
onto my boots and are heading for the sockline, the flesh,
but there is no time to get them off. A Mickey Mouse
Sorcerer's Apprentice situation: by the time I pick them
off, a dozen more will clamber aboard. It is a fix with enough
elements of both nightmare and slapstick comedy to leave me
halfway between tears of rage and tears of laughter.

What would the Geshe do here? I don't know, but I'm
sure he would do the right thing, somehow. Even ordinary
Tibetans seemed to have a natural gift for handing the
difficulties of the world skillfully, gracefully. I once shared a
room in Dharmsala with a young Tibetan man named
Pasang; when I woke the next morning, I was covered with
hundreds of bedbug bites, while he, in his bed a few feet
away, was unscathed. I asked him if he used bug powder,

anathema to most religious Tibetans, who hate to kill anything, and he laughed and said, "No. Tibetans have a deal
with bedbugs. They don't bite us, and we don't kill them."

Luckily, I find out later, leeches are not found everywhere
in the monsoon hills; they favor brushy hillsides at the
4,000-to-7,000-foot level. But that is also quite, quite enough.

All day, onward, up flooded river valley, paddies where
women work in the hip-high water, and the skies roll on,
draining madly onto us all. More blood-engorged leeches drop
from me like dreadful grapes; some burst when they hit the
ground, they are so full of my hemoglobin.

I get to Namdu two hours after dark; again the Mandala
Map is way, way off, displacing the village by miles. The
mapmakers never left Kathmandu, I tell myself: copied it off
some old errant chart whilst under the influence of opiated
hashish, in a Freak Street dosshouse. I curse them all, realiz-
ing as I do how far I am already deviating from my search
for balance, strength, equanimity.

At Namdu the rain is falling like a tidal wave. A farm-
house, a plate of rice, potatoes, and vegetables, and so to bed
on the floor.

The next morning, I hike out through Namdu in a fine,
chilling rain.

It's a long way to Khumbu, Everest; I'm lost among
strangers in bum weather.

I take a bloody defecation, spattered with scarlet, by the
trail: primary sign of amoebic dysentery, which jolts me, as
the cure requires a minimum of two weeks' bed rest, an
obvious impossibility in a land with no beds, no rest, and
me with hardly any money. Still, on I go, picking up a
leech or two along the way.

Checking my map, I decide I will sidetrack an hour or two to Jiri, site of a Swiss aid project, including, supposedly, a guest house for trekkers. I need a break, a day to recoup my energies: culture shock (of a sort), the rain, and the constant climbing and descending are doing me in. I am beginning to have visions, but they are of cheeseburgers and feather beds, turnpikes and supermarkets, television sets and chocolate malts.

Another, usual day: switchbacks up a steep, steep cliff, down into a subvalley, then hours and hours laboring up an 8,250-foot pass, and down a breakneck clay chute to the Sikhri Khola. I fall only ten or twelve times on the descent. Across the river, on a decent footbridge, and up a mountainside of precipitous meadow, fog rolling in now; cattle grazing here and there look like they are floating in the clouds. As I cross a patch of jungle, something green, enormous, whips off a branch onto my arm. I pull at it—it clings frantically. I manage to yank it off and toss it away before it can latch on to me again with its mouth. Shudder. One of the famous Giant Green Leeches, no doubt about it—a bad omen. If that one was any indication, three or four of them, allowed to feed unmolested, could drain off enough blood to kill a healthy trekker. I think I'm getting psyched out—a definite leech complex.

I stumble into Jiri in the late afternoon; past the dirt airstrip, the government buildings—straight, as if by celestial navigation, into the mess hall, where two Jireli women are cooking buttered noodles. It is a relief to come in out of the clouds, the damp, the sneaking cold. At this point, more stress is the farthest thing from my mind; if a helicopter landed and offered me a free ride to Everest, I would probably take it.

It strikes me, as I order up two plates of buttered noodles at five rupees a toss, that I am already losing control and track of things: what began as a would-be pilgrimage is degenerating into an uncomfortable and meaningless forced march to the World's Tallest Tourist Trap. The problem is, I am fudging things; I am just not fanatical enough to do it right. Maurice Wilson was willing to die when he set out for Everest (and what good did it do him?); the Dakota Indians called their vision quests *heniblichia*, meaning, literally, "crying for a vision": utter desperation was necessary to pull the power down. I am just walking—great distances alone in a strange land—but just walking. Perhaps I should burn my last few rupees and go on my way on my hands and knees, pushing a leech-ball with my nose. Perhaps when I get up into the higher altitudes, in the thin air and cold of the big peaks, things will be different.

I don't know. The most extreme modern walk I have ever heard of was the one done by Slavomir Rawicz and six other people, mostly Eastern Europeans, described in Rawicz's out-of-print book, *The Long Walk*. They escaped from Stalinist concentration camps at the end of the Second World War, and trekked south out of the Siberian Arctic, around Lake Baikal, across the Gobi Desert, Sinkiang, the wintry Ch'ang T'ang Plateau of Tibet, finally crossing the main range of the Himalaya into India! At one point in the Gobi they went a solid week without a drop of water; they lived for a month on raw snake meat and putrid water dug out of sump holes. Only two of them survived the journey; during his first two weeks in hospital in India, Rawicz dreamed every night that he was still crossing the wastelands, and was found carrying his mattress up and down the hall!

Obviously, extreme conditions alone don't make the grade.

. . .

Over the next three days I trudge on, thirteen, fourteen, fifteen hours a day: through Chyangma (where I fall in a stream and nearly drown), Sete (where a leech gnaws a huge hole in my hand while I sleep on a mud floor that is a lot more mud than floor), over 12,000-foot Lamjura Pass (ghosts there, the locals warn) to Junbesi, the first real mountain village on my trip. The people are Sherpas, Tibetan stock, with those wonderful broad faces, and there are pine forests and rushing streams (full of dysentery and hepatitis bacilli, I am sure) . . . the kind of scene I came for, dreamed of.

But am I really getting anywhere? I find myself thinking again of the whole *Guinness Book of World Records* syndrome: the idiot attempt to do something, anything, first, best, longest, hardest. Is this what adventuring, that most basic and purest of human endeavors, has sunk to in this benighted age? "If adventure has a final and all-embracing motive," the English climber-explorer Wilfred Noyce wrote, "it is surely this: We go out because it is in our nature to go out, to climb mountains, and to paddle rivers, to fly to the planets and plunge into the depths of the oceans. . . . When man ceases to do these things, he is no longer man." Well, it is rarely so today.

I think of the great adventurers, wanderers, and travelers of the nineteenth and early twentieth century: Doughty, who walked to Mecca and wrote about it in *Arabia Deserta;* Saint-Exupéry, Earhart, Lindbergh, those internal combustion shamans of the sky; Peter Fleming, who traveled overland from Peking to Pakistan in the 1930s, drinking septic water from ditches, dwelling among desert tribes whose tongue he understood nary a word of . . . My own personal favorite is Harry Franck, who after serving in World War I and as a Canal Zone policeman decided to walk the entire length of the Andes. Franck ran out of money, got lost for days on the trackless *altiplano,* extorted food at gunpoint from hostile natives, froze, starved, got sick. When he got down around the southern end of the mountains, Franck turned east and walked all the way across the continent, weeks trudging through knee-deep mud and enduring mosquitoes so vicious that he had to spend his nights running in circles around a smoky fire!

Real noble-madness adventures like Frank's are just about extinct today, thanks to an overorganized, over-mechanized world where long-distance solo rambling is just plain hard to do. Adventuring as an extreme sport has fallen on hard times; everything really good, big, and authentic has already been done, leaving nothing but screwy stunts, the kind they show on Sunday-afternoon television during the dead seasons: a man hanging from a burning rope over a swimming pool full of small blue sharks (really!); another man, no wiser, trying to jump twenty-three sedans on a motorbike in front of a Las Vegas hotel.

Whither the true, powerful deed? I think for some reason of "Bozo" Miller, whom the *Guinness Book of World Records* calls "the world's greatest trencherman." Miller, a 5-foot-7½-inch 290-pounder from Oakland, California (where else?), once ate 27 two-pound pullets at a single sitting; at Oakland's Rendezvous Room, he consumed 324 ravioli, the first 250 in one hour and ten minutes. That train of thought leads me inexorably to the Japanese gentleman who appeared a few years back on Tokyo prime-time TV firing darts out of his posterior into a target; he then, according to my informants, played a Japanese folk tune with that talented orifice.

It strikes me gloomily that my walk to Everest in the rain is kith and kin to this kind of nonsense: "The first man to walk to Chomolungma in monsoon with false teeth made out of bouillon cubes, and less than $23 worth of clothing..." What am I trying to prove, anyway? And to whom? I have no idea at this stage. And what do adventures have to do with visions, anyway? I'm totally confused.

But the real high country is still ahead, of course: the unadorned, hard terrain beyond the forests, where things seem to happen (for me, at least). And this is the highest high country on earth. We shall see, we shall see.

I hike out of Junbesi on a brisk, misting morning. Begin the long climb to Takshindu Pass, at about 10,000 feet. Another hard day ahead, to say the least.

The trail is almost deserted; only a few people with trade goods, spuds, oranges, butter, and such, hiking toward the weekly market in Salleri. I feel a sense of excitement; today I'm going to cross into the Khumbu Valley, the valley of Everest itself, though I will reach the Dudh Khosi River, on the valley floor, at the pitifully low altitude of 4,500 feet. But I feel like I'm almost there. (Of course I'm not.)

In the late morning I take a wrong turn and hike up a really wild and lovely subalpine valley, full of aspenlike trees. Luckily, a mile or so up, I run into a couple of timber cutters who are skidding a big log down the trail, pulling it with ropes. They point back the way I came: "Takshindu, Namche Bazaar," they say. I follow them at high speed as they run down the trail at a breakneck pace, the log skidding after them through the wet, fallen leaves—a mile back down to the main trail. There they stop, and all but physically put me on the trail to Takshindu, pointing repeatedly and saying "Takshindu" over and over again, so that even an idiot like me can't get lost. Hiking up, I look back, and they are still watching me, making sure I stay on the right path. They smile, and nod encouragingly—"Takshindu," they call, and point again. Beautiful people.

The trail switchbacks up. I sweat in the cold air—I must be close to the summit. Just below the top I meet a strange crew coming down: Takshindu Lama, the head of the Takshindu Monastery, a snobbish young incarnate lama; his chief steward, an older, wily-looking individual; followed by a couple of lumpen lamas carrying huge steamer trunks on their heads. They are headed for Kathmandu on business. Eventually, I learn later, the Takshindu Lama hopes to go to America, to go into the wholesale enlightenment racket.

I also hear a funny story about Takshindu Lama from a wandering American ethnolinguist back in Kathmandu. He had spent some weeks at Takshindu Gompa, and while there he sold a pair of thermal long johns to Takshindu Lama for about thirty rupees. The next day he saw another lama proudly wearing the long johns around; inquiring, he learned that Takshindu Lama had resold the long johns to the second lama for several boxes of fine Tibetan tea, a quantity of yak butter, and sixty rupees. A day later he saw another local gent strolling around wearing the top half of the long johns, and yet another wearing the bottoms, lama number two having cleverly cut the long johns in half and resold the halves, at astronomical prices: kilos of tea, brocade, chickens. Never do business with a holy man.

At the summit of the pass I look down on the whole Lower Khumbu Valley spread below, full of clouds and rain. Just below the pass stand the buildings and gardens of the Takshindu Monastery; and below that, a stretch of steep jungle descending into the clouds, beyond which I can see the opposite ridge of the Khumbu Valley miles away: forest, scattered fields, a thin red-brown line of trail. I look up-valley for a glimpse of the big peaks, but cloud and hills are all I see.

I look at the map. It's a long way to Khari Khola, the village where I want to spend the night: a descent of several miles and 5,500 vertical feet to the Dudh Khosi, somewhere down there in the clouds; then a climb of above 2,000 vertical feet and more miles to Khari Khola, amidst those confused, misty subvalleys.

My mind is working like a manic madman's. It's already well past noon, and the daily drizzle is beginning; Khari Khola is a long, long way away; and there are three or four other villages between here and there, no doubt with friendly chai-houses where I could stop well before dark, have a leisurely tsampa and chung . . .

But for some reason I feel I have to make it to Khari Khola—maybe it's the old Guinness complex again: "the first man to make it from Junbesi to Khari Khola in a single day," etc. The same mental hang-up that got me to Nepal in the first place, with no money and less sense. I'll probably pull a Maurice Wilson when I get to Everest: try to solo the icefall in my holey kletters, tumble into a crevasse in a white-out, and never be heard of again.

I tear down the mountain. The trail zigzags through dense jungle, through occasional clearings covered with second growth. I come down into the clouds, into the rain again. The kulis coming up gape at me, madman that I am. Familiar monotones of monsoon, drear and scabrous scenes. Villages hunched in battering rain. Kulis with plastic or rattan over their heads, bent under enormous loads. A silly sahib running down the mountain, knee bleeding where he fell, an apparition in the mist.

I come out into paddy fields and scattered farms. The trail winds and squirms through the paddies, confusing. Grain ricks, a ghastly dead crow hung over them by a rope to frighten away other scavengers. Where am I?

The trail I am on, whatever it is, descends into an evil jungle again. Everything seems ominous. There are no people and no footprints in the mud. The non-sky drizzles on. The more lost I feel, the faster I go. I don't know what time it is.

Then suddenly I come out just above the Dudh Khosi, rushing past in the ravine bottom. The trail drops past dripping cliffs to a suspension bridge. I have come from Takshindu down to the river in about three hours. I get out the map and look at it again. Base Camp is about 18,000 feet, so I've just lost 5,000 feet to gain back 14,000 feet. Discouraging, to say the least. Stupid abstractions fill my head— this reminds me of the old British radio *Goon Show*, where an expedition climbed Everest from the inside (Everest being hollow), but when they got to the top, they had to plant the flag upside down, and it fell out.

I cross the river: on the other side are palm trees, grass shacks; the air is muggy and tropical. I pick up leeches again, a bushel of them.

As evening falls, I find myself trudging up through terraced cornfields, with pitifully poor shacks here and there—this must be a Rai settlement, the Rais being an impoverished Hindu tribe of the lower Dudh Khosi. Ragged, dirty farm women greet me cheerfully, but give vague directions when I ask where Khari Khola is, gesturing in a general upward direction.

The trail I'm on, which must be the wrong one, peters out. Suddenly I am quite lost, on sopping-wet brushy cliffs, thrashing about in the mist. Instead of turning back and trying to retrace my route back to the wrong turn, I keep going. Leeches the size of bush adders lash out at me from every branch and leaf. I crawl up a tricky ridge; the clouds part below, and I'm staring down into a 2,000-foot abyss. That gets the old adrenaline pumping. It's now almost dark, and if I don't find the trail and Khari Khola soon, I'll be dinner for the leeches—this is no place to camp out, for sure.

I push on through swirling fog up the ridge. I come to a high point. There below I see a trail, and beyond it, big farmhouses clustered on a hillside. I have stumbled on Khari Khola.

Bellowing out a Tibetan song in a triumphant atonal semi-quaver, I slog down to salvation through heather and fog. Visibility has shrunk to under a hundred feet when I make it into Khari Khola, get lodging at a convenient house, and start picking the leeches off. One on my foot is the size of a small frog, and a couple of the more resourceful ones have made it into the shelter of my beard.

There *is* a power out here, I am beginning to realize, but I'm not sure it's one I could ever attain, or want to: too hard for me. These hill people are all magi, when you think about it—small as American children and delicate as birds, men and women alike haul one-, two-, even (rarely) three-hundred-pound loads up slippery high-altitude trails again and again and again, all life long. They build houses out of raw stone, hack fields out of cliff faces, tote firewood ten miles to boil water lugged five miles in a leaking jerry can

—pretty magical, as far as I am concerned. Enter a ninety-pound hill woman, one of them I have passed on the trail today, in a fair version of that silly television World's Strongest Man Contest, and she would win it hands down. *Kuli Power*, indeed.

I once heard a story from a big old retired Seabee about something that happened during the Korean War. An ancient Korean man, tiny and frail, showed up at a Seabee camp begging for oil for fuel; the Seabees jokingly told him he could take a whole hip-high drum of it if he could carry it away. They gathered to watch the fun: it took all of one Seabee's strength to get one of those drums tilted with one end an inch off the ground, and three to lift it entirely. Well, the little man, beaming at his benefactors, unslung one of those tumplines rural Asians carry, wrapped one end around his forehead, the other loop around the drum, and adjusted the knot. Squatted down with the drum to his back, humped the huge drum (enough oil for the whole village for a year!) up onto his skinny spine, and went trotting out of camp. The Seabees gaped in astonishment, and then cheered and cheered. Twenty minutes or so later, they saw him in the distance, in the words of my informant, "going up a hill steeper'n a cow's face."

The next couple of days, up to Namche Bazaar, I penetrate deep into the main ranges. It mists and drizzles, and it is colder, vibrations of perma-ice ahead. Milarepa, the Tibetan holy man and poet, traveled these same mountains in the twelfth century. The high passes and peaks he referred to as "No-man's Land," "Snow Country." His poems praise mountains, the wilder the better, as in the example quoted before. On past Namche Bazaar to a monastery high on a tundra ridge, a silver string of river far, far below, human bone clarinets playing those eternal blues, clouds tearing by my boot heels, where I spent long days, weeks, in a whitewashed stone room in the very sky.

I leave the monastery early one morning, heading down the trail into the valley; the trail that turns and leads up again, up and up to Everest, and all the rest. I have a feeling that I have emptied myself out; exhausted, freaked, and otherwise driven myself far enough, so that something, I think— what I am looking for—just may have room to enter me at this last stage of the journey. If the rest of the trip was almost farcical, this last may just do the trick. And it is a fine, dry day; a twenty-pound sack of tsampa and a week's-supply lump of yak butter in my pack, a rolling Tibetan Rolling Stone, I roll on, alone.

Down-valley to Namche Bazaar again, and then up through woods of autumnal yellow; a first good look at Everest, Lhotse, Nuptse, and the rest. Autumn is in the air now; the hillsides are amber where the brush and woods are preparing to drop their leaf.

Past the high twin villages of Khumjung and Kunde and back down to the Dudh Khosi, roaring white in its wild gorge. And up to lovely Thengboche Monastery on its hilltop. Down the fairy-tale valley beyond, auburn moss draped on twisty pines, tiny clear brooks, whitewashed houses in the glens.

I cross the Imja Khola and climb a shrine-studded hillside to Pangboche, where Sherpas are harvesting barley in the stony fields. Now there is snow on the barren ground. I climb above a cobbled valley cut by the stream; houses abandoned for the winter, the people moved to lower elevations, leaving their heavy wooden doors padlocked. Deserted, vision country, I think: nothing growing here now but mystery.

It's a lonely afternoon, through this abandoned country: just the mountains, the trail, and me; and once a solitary Sherpa, driving his firewood-loaded yak toward Dingboche. Here and there on the boulder-strewn mountainsides, huge, half-wild yaks graze through the snow.

In the evening I cross a stony, snowy pass into the next valley. The country below is barren, tundra. To my left, Taboche, a 20,000-footer, turns a cold, delicate red in the sunset; a plume of snow blows off the frozen summit. This is a scene at once beautiful and painful: what the Japanese call *aware*—the transitory beauty of objects, things dying in eternity.

The pass is cold and desolate; the wind howls, tearing at the prayer flags on the summit shrine. I hurry down, crossing the Imja Khola again, turgid with ground-up rock.

At dusk I hike into Pheriche, a summer settlement. Deserted now, its low stone houses are locked up; only one woman has stayed on to put up trekkers, climbers, and porters in a pit-house dug out of the tundra, roofed by a big canvas tent abandoned by the ARGENTINA EVEREST EXPEDITION, the letters say.

Yak jerky, the omnipresent chung, boiled potatoes still bitter with earth. The wind whistles across those barren fields and stone walls as night falls cold at 13,900 feet, a blazing furnace of stars above.

The Mandala Map, as its last boggle, has moved Everest, base camp and all, about fifteen air-miles to one side. But up here there is no problem finding the right trail: there is only one way to go, well-trodden, leading inescapably toward

Everest, the Big One: Chomolungma in Tibetan. Sagarmatha in Nepali.

It is a bright, hot day. The sun pounds down, burning the snow away. I follow the valley up, wading cold melt-water streams. Put my goggles on: today I'll climb to Lobuije at 16,000 feet; with a clear sky and snow on the ground, I don't want to sizzle my eyes.

The trail winds through the open tundra; through Phalang Kharpo, another deserted summer settlement; up around an escarpment to the right, and into the steep terminal and lateral moraines of the icefall.

The moraines are tremendous. The trail goes up a steep boulder field for a long time; on either side are more high rock drifts and, beyond them, mountainsides. There is about a foot of snow on the ground, the unmelted residue of last week's storm, and footing is shifty on the snow-covered scree, except where porters and trekkers have left their tracks.

For about an hour I keep one eye on some riprap rock walls high up ahead in the moraine. That must be Lobuije, I tell myself. But when I finally get there, they are only shrines. Bad cheese, think I.

So I go on through a winding wasteland of junk rock and snow: cutting across the sides of hill-sized screes, plodding on, stovepiping through crust and gnawing greedily at the air, my pack feeling double its forty pounds. Every time I turn a corner and see a big boulder ahead, I flash on it as one of the huts at Lobuije—but it's just another boulder. Hike on through the rock gruntings of the Everest massif: ice and rock oozing down, bleeding out to make all the earth and water and forests of Nepal and India, far below . . . I've come a long, long way.

I sing a tuneless song in time with my breathing—a song

I made up somewhere back on the trail, and that I drone on hard ascents: a song about mountains without color, rivers frozen hard as iron, dancing skeletons of light—eating this Martian air.

In the late afternoon, hiking through cold shadows and fading sun, I come to two rock huts in a dead-end valley, by an iced-up stream: Lobuije.

If I had any thoughts of resting here, they are quickly dispelled by a glimpse at the situation: both drafty, dirt-floored huts are jammed with dozens of Sherpa men and women from a British Everest expedition, a wandering yak herder, a pair of mad hara-kiri Japanese climbers (who have cleverly set up their tent inside one of the huts, ensuring plenty of floor space for themselves), a couple of British trekkers downward-bound from base camp—the whole wild ménage presided over by the hut-keeper, a formidable, rakshi-swizzling Sherpa crone. Colonel Roberts, an old pukka sahib from Kathmandu, and ground liaison man for the British expedition now in the upper icefall, has wisely pitched a tent for himself well away from the huts; there, served by two Sherpa majordomos, he sits in his down bag swigging away at a bottle of Famous Grouse Scotch, in regal splendor.

The sun vanishes behind the icy mountain walls, and immediately the temperature falls about fifty degrees, here at 16,179 feet. The huts settle down to eating (potatoes), farting, shoving for room, jokes and laughter. A greasy young Sherpa who is supposed to be one of the famous Tenzing's myriad sons deliberately drops his pack on my head; his Yahoo friends snicker.

The light goes out. Cramped between a stone wall and a sea of Sherpas, groggily sucking in the thin air, I feel like

I am being compressed in a giant iron mangle. Claustrophobic panics giggle in my skull.

Rats emerge and begin playing rugby across the wall-to-wall bodies. One rat falls into an empty can and spends about ten minutes banging away like a drum before someone chucks a boot at it. Sleep, or an unreasonable facsimile thereof, eventually comes through sheer exhaustion.

I was empty enough, physically and mentally, for ten thousand gods to have entered my mind and body and given me all the powers in this world and the next. Why they didn't, I'll never know.

The moraines went on and on that last day, billions of tumble-stones heaped in mass confusion. Black light battering down. Snow summits flashing in the sun. As I climbed higher and higher, staring up the blue rolling depths of the sky, the moraines fell away on the right. There below was the chaos of the lower Khumbu icefall: mile upon mile of ice, rocks, dust, boulders the size of office buildings, pillars, crevasses that could swallow an army; pools of ice water opal with glacial flour, the bones and excrement of dead mountains, fossil snow, inching down-valley with the power of a million suspended-animation atomic bombs.

The snow was melting on the moraines, water blabbing down the stones. I descended to Gorak Shep, the lake famous in Everest annals, whose name means "Dead Crow." The lake was strewn with small icebergs. The sunlight pounded down with a wearying intensity; the air tasted purple, scorched. I wrapped my head in a shirt, like an Arab *kaffiyeh*.

On and on, up and up . . . On the side of Kala Pattar,

"Black Rock," I sat down to rest, sprawled on the slabs. Everest, Pumo Ri, Lingtren, Lhotse, Nuptse: the highest mountains on earth; holes in the floor of the sky; gods (according to some). Why did people bother to climb them? Why did I? There were no answers.

I was sick of walking, of ascending; sick and tired of the whole trip, in fact. I felt a terrible weariness, a lassitude bordering on inertia (the first symptoms, though I didn't know it at the time, of hepatitis). My thoughts were flying apart, shining smithereens. I felt like I was in a dream, or dreaming that I was in a dream—something like that.

No, no *coup de foudre*. Clouds boiled over the summits; the whole world was burning, like a body on the Ganges *ghats*. A world sired upon a vacuum by the Void, and dying every instant.

I had come high enough. My shoes were falling apart. I was broke, busted. And I had run out of map. I had no desire to go on, up onto those further heights. There was a route I had heard of, off to the right: up over the moraines to a glacier, and up that to a 20,000-foot summit, and over that to the south . . . I had thought of doing it, but now it seemed silly. I didn't want to die up there, and if someone had told me a vision was waiting for me a hundred yards up the trail, I don't think I could have made it up there to find out.

The game was over: I wasn't sure whether I had won, lost, or tied, but it was over. I took one last look around, at the cold, white ranges and started back down.

An afterword is definitely in order.

Two weeks after I set out for Everest, two women I had met in India, call them Joanna and Francesca, started on the same long trek. It was raining harder, if anything: the trails with hazardous drop-offs, bridges gone, leeches . . . dreadful.

This is the story Joanna told me a month later back in Kathmandu: "The fourth day out, we were walking in the early morning. It was raining so hard we could barely see a hundred feet in any direction. I had gone on ahead of Francesca, and I came to a stream. It was moving really fast and there was no bridge, just a series of stones. You had to jump from one to the next. I got out in the middle, and then I just froze. The next stone was just too far to jump to, and I was slipping. Once in the water, I would have been swept away, drowned—

"Suddenly a bearded man, a saddhu, appeared beside me; he was wading in the water, bracing himself on a long wooden staff. He spoke to me in perfect English, that funny kind of accented English educated Indians speak. 'Here, let me help you,' he said. He took my arm and helped me the rest of the way across the stream.

"I sat down on a rock, real shaky still from almost falling in the water. A minute later, Francesca came across the stream to where I was. 'It's a good thing that saddhu helped me,' I said. 'What saddhu?' Francesca asked. I looked around and there was no one there.

" 'I watched you cross the stream,' Francesca said. 'There was no one else there. You started to lose your balance in the middle, and then, after a few moments, you pulled it all together. I tried to call to you, but the sound of the water was too loud. But there was no one out there with you.' "

6

Shamanism opened up some avenues of exploration; but because I did not understand the triggering device, how these responses could be made repetitive, they seemed to fall short.

There was another approach, however, roundabout but workable. In my research I found that biochemists were beginning to work on analyzing the mechanisms of shamanism and similar phenomena. Shamanistic initiations, athletic ecstasies, and the like are, after all, biochemical, whatever else they might be: something actually happens, in the meat of the body, a process involving the endorphins, adrenaline, and all the other chemicals that make us do well or poorly or not at all at whatever difficult things we try and do.

The search for scientific sources proved in its own way to be as difficult as the physical searches I had already made. The information was out there, but for the most part in the obscurest and most esoteric of journals, and in research just beginning to find its way into print: the scholarly equivalent of the mountaintops and deserts, the drastic risks and edges of endurance, of the other side of the quest.

It was almost as if there were some kind of spell on the really vital information, making it, if not hard to get, at least intriguingly squirreled away in this or that obscure academic niche. To get one treatise I had to write the Royal Naval Librarian in England; to get another chunk of information, I had to send a blank tape to an experimental psychologist in Canada with a list of questions and wait for him to send it back with the recorded answers. I computer-searched the library at the National Institutes of Health, and traveled in mid-winter on the slowest train in Christendom to the tip of Long Island for a middle-of-the-night meeting with Dr. Andrew Weil. A weird search, indeed.

Begin at the beginning, with what I found.

Nerve cells communicate with one another through messages, messages in the form of amino acids and complex chains of amino acids called peptides. Amino acid messages are simple, on the order of yes/no, an on/off switch; a peptide, like a complex sentence, may contain whole strings of information. Either way, the messaging process is remarkable. In the words of Dr. Murray Saffran, "The message must leave the cell of origin, pass into the blood, attach itself to a specific blood protein, which then carries it to a specified organ, where the message leaves the blood protein, attaches to a particular cell, and tells that cell to start to manufacture a certain product." To make the process even more ornate, the amino acid or peptide messenger can deliver its message only by entering the cell. Nerve cells are designed like locked boxes: entry is via chemical doors, or receptor sites, and only the correct chemical key will unlock a particular receptor site: adrenaline must enter through the adrenaline site, serotonin through the serotonin, etc.

The body's response to stress situations, the kind one finds in the hardest of games, is orchestrated by a whole complex set of chemical messages between the nerve cells, keys in locks, calls and responses. Initially a hormone biochemists call Big ACTH (for adrenocorticotropic hormone) is released; as it breaks down, it gives birth to a wide spectrum of potent substances, each of which does something or things to mobilize the body and mind.

Beta-endorphin seems to be the prime mover in the stress biochemistry equation: "It stands right at the center of the control network," according to biologist Derek Smyth, "able to produce analgesia or even catatonia, to lower blood sugar, to modulate by inhibition the brain's established neuro-transmitters, and to stimulate the release of a host of pituitary hormones that in themselves play critical roles in behavior." The story behind the discovery of endorphin is a particularly interesting one, a real piece of scientific detective work. Neurobiologists researching narcotics addiction found receptor sites on nerve cells that fit exogenous (that is, from outside the human body) opiates like opium, morphine, and heroin. How, they asked, could such sites have evolved when man has only used opiates for the past three or four thousand years? (The opium poppy, *Papaver somniferum*, was probably first used, medicinally and/or recreationally, on the eastern shores of the Mediterranean during the Neolithic.) There must be endogenous substances, secreted by the human body itself, that fit into those same receptor sites, similar in form and function to the opiates. And there were, the neurobiologists found: beta-endorphin, and similar, somewhat less potent peptides called enkephalins.

Getting back to the stress response, beta-endorphin's most dramatic role is as a painkiller; tests have shown it to have a hundred times the analgesic power of morphine. Enkephalins, on the other hand, in addition to being analgesics, help modulate the mood-altering chemicals like serotonin, dopamine, norepinephrine (noradrenaline), and epinephrine (adrenaline): you could say that they help reestablish and maintain emotional equilibrium. Interestingly, beta-endorphin can be split into two Jekyll and Hyde component chemicals, alpha-endorphin and gamma-endorphin. It is the former that produces the euphoria and analgesia, the bliss and the lack of pain; gamma-endorphin has been shown, in tests on laboratory animals, to induce quite the opposite effects: irritability, excitability, increased sensitivity to pain. In stress and survival situations, the two complement one another: enough alpha to deal with the pain and fear, and enough gamma to keep you in touch with the realities of the situation so that you can react correctly.

But there is more to the biochemical stress equation than just endorphins and enkephalin. Big ACTH also contains a kind of "small" ACTH that acts as a trigger for stimulating chemicals like epinephrine (adrenaline) and norepinephrine (noradrenaline), whose effects include increased mental awareness, muscle rigidity, heightened senses. And there is also MSH (melanocyte-stimulating hormone) in the Big ACTH catalogue, a substance that has been found to hype alertness and accelerate the learning process in laboratory animals. This last probably explains the tales so many disaster survivors tell, of their lives flashing before them like a speeded-up film: the biocomputer of the brain is doing an accelerated search through its memory banks, looking for the bit of information that will provide a way out of the fix. And more: when the body goes into oxygen debt, as it does after heavy exertion, the carbon dioxide levels rise; carbon dioxide breaks down into lactic acid, a known cause of altered states of consciousness. Dehydration, plummeting blood sugar levels—the range of chemical stress consequences is practically endless.

What does all this mean in terms of searching for peak performances and experiences in sports, or anything else that pushes the human animal to the limit? Practically everything. It seems as if the two, biochemistry and performance, are directly linked: when the biochemistry is good, the performance and the experience are good; when it is bad, they are bad.

For instance, Big ACTH can decompose in a great many ways, producing more or less of this or that chemical. Say you get too much adrenaline and noradrenaline, and not enough of the ameliorating, nonstimulating chemicals: the results can be panic, hysteria. I remember climbing an easy 200-foot crack in the cliffs west of Boulder, Colorado, a route I had done many times before, that ended in a lovely little bonsai fir tree stuck in the sandstone face like Excalibur; I used to sit up there, back against the rock, feet braced against the gnarled wood, and look out over the world. This time, halfway up, a rock the size of my head fell out of nowhere, smashed against the cliff not six feet from my left hand, and bounded away into the Void below. It all happened so fast I didn't have time to think about it, but in the next few seconds I found myself filling up with senseless, abject terror. My hands gripped the rock till my fingers turned gray; the strength drained out of my legs. I felt sick to my stomach; I was completely unmanned (a perfect word). It took me twenty minutes to work up the nerve to move one muscle, and then another, and to begin to climb down the hundred feet to the highest grassy ledge; the easiest of climbs, but suddenly it was dreadfully hard, almost more than I could handle. My mind was blank, numb. I realize now that what I had was a bad case of adrenaline poisoning; somehow the reactive juices had flown foul, wrong. When I got to the bottom I was drenched in sweat, shaking uncontrollably.

On the other hand, too much beta-endorphin and not enough of the rest can put you into a zombie-like trance, shock, a junkie's nod, like the surrendered gazelle that turns its throat up to the ravenous lion. I have had that happen, too; working heavy construction in Boulder, 1973, when a 300-pound concrete slab free-fell two and a half feet onto my left foot, catching the great toe as I tried to leap out of the way. I instantly went into a kind of woozy dream state. I leapt down from the flatbed truck and began walking around in tight little circles, saying, "I'm fine. Really. No problem. I'll be okay in a minute. Just a nick." I even laughed, a sound, my fellow workers told me later, that was one of the most horrible any of them had ever heard. When I finally sat down against a wall and pulled my shoe off—I was wearing thin rock-climbing shoes, in direct violation of company, state, and union rules—and poured a cup's worth of blood out, it still didn't connect. I couldn't feel a thing; my toe felt the way your tooth does after it's been drilled down to the root, and the Novocain is just beginning to wear off; numb, dumb, with faint tintinnabulations of aching somewhere out there in the emptiness. Even when I pulled the sock off and saw the blanched, bruised thing that had been a toe, it was like looking at a film of someone else. Is that me? Misshapen, blood squirting from the cracks, the nail a glorious purple-black? It might have been a satellite transmission from Mars. I talked Joycean nonsense all the way to the emergency room in the cab of the pickup. "Great day. Aspens must be turning any day now up at ten thousand . . . My girlfriend should be back by Friday . . . Is that one of those new BMWs? Why do they call the town 'Boulder'?—" I think I felt, somewhere inside, that if I stopped talking the pain would come bursting in; the words formed a kind of wall of normalcy, business as usual. They x-rayed my toe at the emergency room and found that both bones had been completely broken, both across and lengthwise; in fact, there wasn't enough of anything solid left in there to put back together. They scrubbed the smashed digit with betadyne—the nail simply fell off the moment the rag touched it—wrapped it in gauze, wrote me a prescription for thirty Tylenol No. 3, q.i.d., and sent me home. The next day I was back on the job. Limping around in agony, when the pain finally did arrive. A couple of hours after the accident, it came on full bore, popping the cold sweat out of my forehead and squeezing my voice into a thin squeak when the worst throbs hit.

Sometimes, though, the chemistry is right. More often it is less than completely right but still not bad, and sometimes it is an utter, dysfunctional disaster: if I had had to *do* anything to save myself when my toe was crushed—if it had happened in a rockfall in the remote mountains instead of a crowded construction site—the same shock that deadened my pain and knocked me so silly would probably have deadened me, too. Ditto my adrenaline rush on the climb—on a harder pitch, I would have chickened myself straight into oblivion.

The stress response can manifest itself in all kinds of negative ways. Distance runners, for instance, actually seem to get hooked on the endorphin-rich biochemical response kindled by their sport. "Not only do marathon runners get high off endorphins, they become dependent on them," says Dr. Andrew Weil. "It *is* an addiction. I've seen a number of such runners who, when they are prevented from running for a day or two, become really unpleasant to be around." Indeed, statistical studies show that upwards of 20 percent of competitive runners are forced to seek professional psychiatric help, occasionally to the point of being institutionalized, when injuries interrupt their running activities for significant periods of time.

The same kind of addiction to stress biochemistry, though I suspect in this case the prime addictive agent is adrenaline rather than endorphin, seems to afflict the risk-taking athletes, the speed skiers, hang-glider flyers, big-wave surfers, and the rest; and it explains the crazed, incessant, febrile atmosphere that clings to these athletic scenes. Certain Shoshoni Indians, when they want a real, insensate high, have what they call dynamite parties; they take turns lying in a hole in the ground, and having dynamite charges set off a few feet away; the blast blows them right out of the hole, and they come down, sprawling, in some kind of weird state of *ekstasis*. The extreme sports scene has a lot more in common with dynamite parties than it does with shamanistic initiation or Zen meditation or any of the other disciplines that aim at controlling and texturing one's own responses to the stresses of the world. Mind-blown pleasure is a long, long way from reacting perfectly, inevitably, to everything the universe throws at you, an easy waltz with danger or death itself.

Back to the subject at hand. Is it unreasonable to suggest that shamans actually control their own biochemical responses to stress and can invoke the precisely right endocrinal mix at will? Canadian psychologist Dr. Raymond Prince suggests just this possibility in a 1980 paper titled "Shamans and Endorphins: Exogenous and Endogenous Factors in Psychotherapy." He writes of an optimum physical/psychological state that springs out of what he calls the "omnipotence maneuver," a feeling of being in absolute, perfect control of a dangerous situation, and indeed, all situations. Prince believes that the body's endocrinal response to stress is at the root of this feeling. Do shamans learn to trigger this response in themselves and then to pass it on to their disciples via ritualized stress situations, carefully engineered crises? It certainly makes sense; and it pulls together such disparate items as my experience on Mount Neva, M'Ikiara's Mount Kenya climb, and the young wizard Tenzing's impossible gymnastics on the Zatr Og.

Dr. Prince writes: "in a situation of life stress . . . a state of hyper-arousal occurs which generates appropriate endorphins or other neuroendocrines in such quantities that an unprecedented feeling of cosmic peace and tranquility is experienced." Certainly that state of mind (and body) is the kind that produces great performances; when you feel totally relaxed yet absolutely involved in the task at hand, your actions and reactions are at their absolute best. And if someone could put himself or herself into that state at will (which shamans and their ilk seem to be capable of doing), they would appear to the rest of us as supermen and -women. Human beings can actually hit that same perfect pitch sometimes through simple practice, practice, practice, controlling the normally uncontrollable; consider that splendid question supposedly addressed by Shirley Temple, at the age of ten, to a movie director: "When I cry, do you want the tears to run all the way down my face, or should I stop them halfway?"

Another, peripheral idea: do shaman types somehow become biochemically *different*, superior, after a time; do they in effect evolve themselves into physically different beings? This would account for a whole host of beliefs found around the world. K'ung Bushmen believe that the perspiration of shamanistic trance dancers contains magical properties; that if you rub the dancers' sweat on your own body, it will ward off illness and weakness. In Tibet, the mummified flesh of long-dead saints is made into pills, which sell for as much as $500 in gold apiece; you take the pill and supposedly go into twenty-four hours of enlightenment, in which you feel and think and perceive the world exactly as it is—the perfect bliss that surpasseth understanding. A direct transfusion, communion of fossilized Nirvana: food (pardon the pun) for thought.

Some modern scientific experiments seem to confirm that shamans and similar characters can indeed control those bodily functions normally considered uncontrollable, including the neuroendocrine system.

In 1960 Indian doctors sealed a Hindu holy man named Shri Ramanand Yogi in an airtight box and observed him and his bodily functions; Ramanand claimed that he had previously been buried underground for up to twenty-eight days at a time, and the physicians wanted to find out if he really could decrease his basal metabolism and oxygen use at will. The results were quite interesting: while confined in a six-by-four-by-four-foot glass and metal box, once for eight hours, another time for ten, Ramanand accomplished the seemingly impossible: his oxygen use dropped from 19.5 liters an hour to 13.3, with none of the usual symptoms of lack of oxygen. The limbic portion of the brain, which regulates the body's endocrinal and other autonomic activities, does not normally respond to conscious commands; it operates on a purely instinctual, involuntary level. In Shri Ramanand's case, he was evidently able to command the limbic part of his brain, the part that usually remains impervious to direct orders, to reduce his body's need for oxygen, below the parameters of what is supposed to be humanly possible. The implications of this, as far as my own search for the athletic Golden Mean, were tremendous.

In another experiment in 1982, Dr. Jeffrey Hopkins and a group of American and Indian physicians confirmed that Tibetan lamas can cause their surface body temperatures to rise as much as 15 degrees in an hour through sheer "willpower." The Tantric Buddhists of Tibet have traditionally practiced a kind of yoga called *tummo;* according to Tibetan texts, an adept can push the surface temperature of his body up so high that he can sit on the snow-covered ground in midwinter and melt holes all the way through to the bare soil, or can dry out water-soaked sheets wrapped around him. In the 1982 experiment, temperature-sensitive devices were attached to the bodies of *tummo* practitioners on the calf, navel, palm, toe, and other spots. The monks then went into their heat-producing meditation; surface skin temperatures rose an average of 10 degrees Fahrenheit on the fingers and 11 degrees on the toes, while the temperature deep in the lamas' bodies remained around the normal 98.6 degrees.

Experiments with biofeedback over the past few years have shown that everyday, average, modern human beings can learn to control some of the same functions of the autonomic* nervous system that yogis and shamans can. Blood pressure, for instance. If blood pressure is made visible via an oscilloscope or graph, subjects quickly learn to control it; perhaps they don't really understand how they are controlling it, but they are; by "thinking the right thoughts," putting themselves in the proper frame of mind, they can lower their blood pressure far more effectively naturally than by any of the blood pressure drugs currently on the market. In another set of experiments, most notably by Berkeley brain researcher Joe Kamiya in San Francisco, subjects were taught to control their own brain wave patterns, producing at will more alpha rhythms (the electrical rhythm associated with meditation, relaxation, etc.). When alpha rhythms were being produced, a bell or tone sounded; subjects tried to keep the tone going, thereby gaining more and more control over their own mental functioning. In other, later experiments, test subjects learned to control the beta and theta electrical activity of their brains also.

So far experiments on self-control of biochemistry have not reached such levels of sophistication; the amounts of the various endocrinal components in the stress chemistry equation are very small, and difficult to quantify. The promise

* The autonomic nervous system regulates, among other things, the cardiovascular, respiratory, and endocrine systems. In the words of Dr. Weil, "it carries out its functions without our being aware of it. Moreover, if we try to will an autonomic response . . . in the same way that we will a movement of our arm, we do not have much success."

is there, however. We already know that certain kinds of exertion produce certain biochemical reactions; mountain runners, tested before and after a trial run, showed a 200 percent average increase in their base beta-endorphin levels. What we are discovering in our games, and what shamans, yogis, and lamas seem to have known intuitively for thousands of years, will undoubtedly become the stuff of laboratory experiments.

In the meantime, the combined information I had put together on shamanism and biochemistry was encouraging, to say the least: it seemed to confirm that there was an actual bodily process going on, and one that could perhaps be controlled.

What I could do, I decided, was this: keep looking for scientific answers while trying to apply what I learned to my actual game-playing experiences.

For instance: if in a certain sports situation I got a stress response I could identify as mostly adrenaline, and in another sports situation a response that was mostly endorphin, perhaps I could fine-tune a stress situation that combined the two into that Golden Mean. Or if I encountered another Neva-like experience, I could pay more attention to the actual circumstances that set it off, analyzing them in biochemical terms: preternatural calms, moments of hysteria, feelings of bliss, that corresponded with known biochemical consequences of stress. Perhaps through trial and error I could put together something like the shaman's trigger mechanism on my own.

7

Perhaps thinking about those perfect stress reactions was the catalyst for what happened next: another encounter, almost accidental, but strong, with the power I had found on Neva. Autosuggestion perhaps, but does that really make it any less valid or remarkable? I'll take my power where I find it, thank you.

I got into it while I was living back east, in Arlington, Virginia, recuperating from another year of misadventure in Asia. One of those blank spaces, bubbles, that form in the flow of one's life; empty time, empty pockets, empty dance card, nothing to do and far too much time to do it in. Looking back on it, I think I was right on the edge of what the British so eloquently call "Going round the Bend." Running appeared in that gray emptiness like an angel; I could have just as easily fallen in love or found Jesus or started chanting "Nam-ho renge-kyo!"

I ran. Alone, because I didn't know anyone to run with. Before dawn, because I wanted to avoid the stultifying heat

and humidity of Virginia summer days. Great, fanatical distances, because there was nothing else going on in my life,
no reason to stop, no one and nothing waiting for me at the
imaginary finish line. By August I was doing two and a half
hours a day, past sunup, into the edge of the black heat and
the pounding light. Strange times, beyond exhaustion: inadvertently my running had that out-of-bounds quality that
makes for powerful experiences.

A typical run began at five A.M. I woke in darkness to the
shrill cry of the alarm, got into my shorts, T-shirt, Adidas,
socks, and sweatband (a torn-up bandana), ate a doughnut
for energy, and went out the door, out to the street. It was
foggy, the streetlight blooming halos, the parked cars silver
with fallen mist. Air heavy as flannel. I trotted the length of
North Edison Street and turned right at the corner, south
down Williamsburg Boulevard, into the endless suburbs.

The beginning of every run was always the same: dreadful. Why was I out there, anyway? Those first half-dozen or
ten, twenty blocks, it felt like someone had injected damp
sand into my hip joints, beneath my kneecaps. I felt like
number six and a half of the seven ages of man, graceless,
creaky, and weak. I wanted nothing more than to turn
around and go home, tumble into bed, go back to sleep. (I
never did: why, I have no idea.)

Climbing the first long, rolling hills (east, south, west,
then south again), I remembered every unpleasant run I had
ever done in the past. The high school gym classes where you
circled a cinder track in the rain like a rat on a treadmill,
spitting tobacco ashes and feeling unutterable teenage gloom;
prep school football, sweating in pads and helmet, the whistle
whipping us back and forth down the field, wind sprints in
the September heat until your tongue felt like a strip of jerky

and your calves cramped up solid; ski workouts in the hills above Boulder, Colorado, up trails so steep that in places you had to pull yourself up with your hands, up through the wet rocks and tree roots.

"When the going gets tough, the tough get going," the coaches used to say; and, "Nobody ever drowned in sweat." Oh? I'm not so sure. When the going gets tough, the smart get going, out of where the going is tough: so I told myself as I huffed and puffed up over Minor Hill in the dark. And who *wants* to drown in sweat? It sounded like a torment from one of Hieronymus Bosch's really sick infernos, with some people being lowered into vats of warm perspiration while others have their tongues stretched out on the ground and plowed and others are sautéed in skillets. Who wanted, who needed it? Not me. But I kept on going. Always.

"You have to go through hell to get to heaven," a friend of mine used to say. By the time I came down the far side of Minor Hill, into the second ten minutes, I began to feel better. I was falling into a rhythm; my stride eased and lengthened out, my arms lost their jerky motion. Down into the network of streets to the north, and back around the flank of the hill to the dew-sodden playing fields of Williamsburg Junior High School. Out onto the trackless turf.

I didn't know how long one of those laps was—a third of a mile, three-eighths; it didn't totally matter. I ran one and then another and another, sometimes varying the routine by cutting off to circle the whole school, dropping down onto the grassy slopes at the field's edge: three laps, five, seven, ten, knocking out the distance. I didn't wear a watch when I ran back then; I wasn't racing anyone or anything. I thought timing a run was a disease, something like carving notches on the bedpost to record lovers. Perhaps I was right.

I ran the Williamsburg fields a long, long time, my feet bouncing up starry showers of dew from the long grass. The sky turned gray, glowing, a streak of red to the east, over Washington. On and on. One last, looping circuit, sprinting along the southern edge, and I turned off onto the street and into the steep wooded neighborhoods that led down to Old Dominion Run. The trees roofed the road, thick as jungle. Down those lovely curves and chacanes, and across Old Dominion, dodging the first commuter cars of the day. Runners were rare on the East Coast back then: I felt like the last of the Mohicans, Ishi, Mister Montagnard, the ghost of a Neolithic hunter, skipping past those sinister machines, down into the narrow roads along Little Pimmit Run. I half-expected gunfire. (Later, when runners were numerous enough to be threatening, rednecks would curse and gesture obscenely from their pickup trucks: quite rightly, as all rednecks are John Wayne at heart, and runners are Crazy Horse incarnate.)

By now I was getting into the really good stuff, what I called, in my mind, "The Float." Some days it was stronger, better than others, but I always found it out there. It wasn't what I ran for exactly, but I doubt I would have kept running so hard, so assiduously, if it hadn't been there.

My blue Adidas felt like they were barely touching the ground; my shins cleaved the air as if in a dream, my hands grabbed off great masses of space and cast them aside. I felt I could run forever. Second wind, third wind, fourth . . . how many winds were there? Travelers in old Tibet told of encountering yogis called *lung-gom-pa*, who traveled in leaps thirty feet long and half as high, as if they had swallowed a kangaroo whole, crossing from horizon to horizon in a few minutes. In 1924, Ernest Thompson Seton met a Tarahumara

Indian postman in northern Mexico who trotted seventy miles a day, seven days a week, with a heavy mail sack, over mountains and barrancas. There *are* no limits.

Flushed with blood, oxygen, and mindless joy, I climbed the fierce hills below Jamestown School as if they weren't there. Leaping the curbs for the sheer delight of it, racing out onto the turf of Jamestown field . . . I rode that inscrutable power through the last hour of the run, impossibly fast, around and around the field, down the long sidewalks to Yorktown High School a mile away (too much traffic by now to run the streets), two or three laps around the football field—"The Float," indeed—and up the last hill to North Edison Street, in the cadmium light of the risen sun, pulling my long, spidery shadow with me down that last block, totally out of breath, arms pumping, feet flying, a final leap to crash on the front lawn at the end; lying there, staring up into the sky, gone, gone, totally gone . . .

Somehow, I was quite literally outrunning myself. Even in the best of my younger days, I had never been anything as a distance runner: too stocky, bones as heavy as stone, short legs. I had trouble with anything over a two- or three-mile trot, and I didn't enjoy it at all. Now, thirty-three years old, with a bad knee and toe smashed up in that construction accident and never really healed, I was racing far greater distances than I had ever imagined possible, with supernatural ease. One day, out of curiosity, I got out a street map of the Northern Virginia suburbs, and carefully traced my usual running route with one of those calibrated pencil-like devices that roll across maps and tote up mileage. I found I was running close to nineteen miles a day, two hours and fifteen, twenty minutes, seven days a week; something strange was going on.

In some ways it reminded me of what the Chinese Taoists call *wu wei*, "doing without doing": you let an action—meditating, ruling an empire, running—"do" itself, without interference, and thereby achieve a perfection impossible to plan or contrive at. "The best runner leaves no tracks," the *Book of Tao,* the *Tao Te Ch'ing,* says: consumed by the act, borne away on the kamikaze, the divine wind. And Zen also: "When you do something, do it completely; don't do anything else. When you chop wood, just chop wood."

Somehow I had stumbled on the trigger mechanism or something like it, I thought. I was doing the impossible, really, day after day, time after time; and the feeling was very, very close to the feeling I had gotten on Neva: slightly different, probably because the games and their difficulties were different, but that same feeling of near omnipotence, bliss, and a kind of wordless, intuitive insight into the world of things around me.

The feeling persisted, for the most part, when I moved back to Colorado, to the little mountain town of Telluride, that fall. I kept on running alone, hewed close to that stringent but rich life I had discovered. The jump in altitude, from near sea level to almost nine thousand feet, threw me off at first, but I stayed with it: not as far or as long, but still catching those transcendences.

My favorite runs were the wildest ones, on the old mining roads that led deep into the mountains above town. Bear Creek: along the willowy banks of the San Miguel River, across it on the wooden bridge (looking down into the molten glass water, the polished cobbles of the riverbed incandescing like hot coals), and up the first steep grade, where avalanches roared down from above in the spring; turning south, up into the narrow valley of Bear Creek, through deep timber and meadows. There were places where snowmelt ran down across the road in little streams, and I splashed through. The last butterflies of the season fluttered over the meadow grasses as if they could soak up a winter of life from the sun itself; Vladimir Nabokov hunted butterflies here back in the fifties. Stands of quaking aspen, sulfur and orange leaves rattling like fire, the cold white roar of the stream—a vibrant country. I loped up that dirt road through the wilderness, wishing I could live forever, the road could roll on forever, this running never stop. Already I felt a strange, sad premonition that this was too good to be true, to last.

Another, shorter run went up the face of the ski mountain itself: steep, so steep that in places I couldn't really run, had to travel in a comical-looking series of galumphs, arms flailing to keep me going. Ten minutes up, and I was looking down on the town as if I were in a glider; I could spit and just about hit my own chimney. There were huge boulders here and there in the forest, fragments of an accidental Stonehenge or Rollright Stones; sometimes I stopped to do climbs on them, twenty or thirty feet on the nearly sheer sides, in the dank druidic gloom. Then off, and further up, through boggy grass, to the bizarre rock turrets called Camel's Garden. They were stranded in the sky on a high ridgeline. I used to sit up there catching my breath, watching the autumn clouds drizzle on the valley below; and then run down, in great kangaroo leaps, almost losing it on the muddy turns, racing down into the streets of town.

Sometimes, for the pure speed of it, I ran on the highway west of town, three miles out to the intersection and three miles back in something like thirty-eight minutes. Almost dead flat, through the horse pastures of the old rancher nicknamed Alley Oop, below the roan cliffs; Turkey Creek Mesa to the left, Last Dollar and Milk to the right, and high mountains beyond. There was little traffic; it was peaceful out there. I saw marmots, coyotes, and once a golden eagle who followed me for nearly two miles, its uranium eye fixed on me like a mad mesmerist's as it soared low over the fencelines.

Autumn went on and on that year; in fact it lasted almost the entire winter. It was the year of the Great Western Drought: a freak high-pressure area settled over the Basin, blocking the blizzards that usually rolled across from the Pacific. An eerie unseason, with balmy chinook winds, dry turquoise skies, and nights of inexplicable blue moonlight, kindled out of the desiccated ice crystals drifting in the troposphere, I suppose. The ski area was still closed in January. There was just enough snowpack to block the back roads, but I kept on running, on the highway; when I felt particularly loose and strong, I ran all the way up to Farney's Ranch and back, ten miles, with a grueling hill climb up the face of Turkey Creek Mesa. Fine stuff. Running to get these same ecstasies I had found in Virginia.

As the winter wore down into spring, something began to happen to my running. The element of mindless joy burned out; I found the sport more and more of a task, something I had to force myself to do. The speed and the effortlessness, the feeling I could tango on air, began to go, too. I had fallen in love, or a reasonable facsimile of, that January, and I really think that had something to do with it. Perhaps the gods who rule lone runs and other hard deals, who pass out the ecstasies and revelations, felt I had broken my bargain with them. Or, to put it another way, loneliness contributes to the physical and psychological equation that squeezes peak experiences out of stress, and when it goes, so do the joys. Through the fall and early winter I had been living the same kind of solitary life I did back east, where my vision runs began: a rented room in a Victorian hovel full of ski bums, a night job diving for pearls at a local restaurant, part-time day work laying pipe on a dirt road up Last Dollar Mesa, an occasional ski mountaineering expedition up on the thin snows of Greenback, Mendota, El Diente ("The Fang") . . . a dreamlike, lonely existence in which my swift runs through a shining landscape resonated like songs shouted down a deserted valley.

Now love, or whatever it was, had entered my life, and as the woman became more and more important to me, the magic in my running faded. The easy speed fled; I grunted and wheezed over the roads and trails where I had flowed, biting off small blue chunks of air and spitting them out like feathers, only a few weeks before. I saw it happening, and there was nothing I could do about it. I looked the same, but inside I was different. The grease was gone from my lightning.

Finally I reinjured my left knee. I had smacked it on a rock above Boulder, Colorado, back in 1973, knocking something loose. Now, running down the slithery Bear Creek road in a cold rain, I slipped, made a wild, slewed leap to keep from falling into the steep forest below, and landed hard, with a crunch. It felt like someone had fired a load of buckshot beneath the kneecap. I was laid up for nearly a week, and when I started up with my running again, there was a hitch in my gitalong. I found myself running in a kind of high-speed limp. My body, which had felt like a slim envelope of fine translucent muscles, suddenly felt clumsy,

heavy as lead, gloom running through its veins mingled with
thick, dark blood.

There is a peculiar, diseased idea in the West that if you do
something wrong hard enough, it will somehow come out all
right. It was the idea behind the worst excesses of the Viet-
nam War and a tremendous amount of popular modern
American culture (including, remember, the mad side of
the extreme sports movement); and it was the idea that
came to me now. I would screw it on, would run so hard and
far that I would smash my way back into the state of grace.

I decided to run the Pikes Peak Marathon that August:
that, I thought, would do it—7,748 vertical feet, fourteen
miles, up to a 14,110-foot summit, and another fourteen
miles back down to the bottom. Extreme enough, I thought.
And Trujillo, that most magical of runners, ran it (of course,
his best runs were done alone, without competition . . . but
I wasn't thinking).

Through the warm, drowsy days of summer, I trained
desultorily, running two or three times a week. Not bad runs,
but nothing like the intensity of the old ones. A page from
my notebook of those days:

Sunday: I run almost to the old ghost town of Tomboy and back.
2½ hours, 2,000 vert. feet, 6–7 miles up (?)—ran down in 40
minutes, as strange birds whistled from the timberline brush and
a cloud of butterflies surrounded me. On the narrow stretch by
the waterfall, feelings of vertigo as I stare down ghastly 70-degree
gullies into thinnest air . . .

I don't know why nothing came of these runs, in the transcendence department; but nothing did. Things had changed;
I didn't know why then, but they had.

Pikes Peak lies just to the west of Colorado Springs, on the very edge of the Rockies, where the Great Plains begin. It took me six hours of driving to get there, over three hundred miles of mountain and basin; a real grind of a drive, on twisting roads in the too-bright sun. Exhausting work: is there anything more wearying than a long drive? And is there anything more incongruous than driving to a run? It seemed silly to me, unnatural, and vaguely irritating.

I arrived in Colorado Springs in the evening and drove out to the canyon suburb of Manitou Springs, starting point for the race. Checked into a motel, ate dinner at a nearby café, went back to the motel and tried to get some sleep. It wasn't easy in the usual swampy motel bed, the room with that weird motel smell, like the dug-up floor of the Sea of Salesmen. A series of violent electrical storms rolled through during the night, with deafening drumrolls of thunder and lightning flashes that lit up the room like high noon. I didn't get more than two hours of sleep in all.

At 7:00 A.M. the streets were still wet and there was a queasy, sulfurous light to the east. I went outside and looked west: the summit of Pikes bore a dusting of new snow, and storm clouds sagged from the ridges.

I ate breakfast—chocolate cake for the carbohydrates, coffee for the caffeine jump—and walked over to the starting area. I had never been around the competitive running scene before; well, here it was in all of its splendor. A thousand-odd upper-middle-class (for the most part) Americans, flexing their calves, twisting themselves into yogic pretzel shapes, gobbling rainbows of vitamins, anti-inflammatories, and muscle relaxants, and talking in a kind of buzz-word code. "Had trouble with shin splints till I got these custom orthotics—" "It's Coca Bee Pollen, and it really got my times down—" "Personal best was a three forty-one fifteen in Denver—" "The old New Balances weren't as good as the Brooks, but the uppers didn't rip out after a hundred clicks, either—" "You're either the psycher-out, or the psych*ee*, and I make it a rule never to—" Etcetera, etcetera, ad infinitum, ad nauseam. Why did I find it so instantly alienating? I don't know what I had expected—a few dozen high-altitude Zen monkeys in black canvas high-tops and Inca skullcaps, chewing peyote buttons—but this wasn't it. I guess I had thought all the runners would be like Rick Trujillo, that mysterioso Pikes Peak champion I had gotten to know a few years back: silent, fairly oozing integrity, The Runner with No Name. Well, it weren't so. The air was full of egomaniacal ravings and, just as bad, equipment-freak soliloquizing. What shoe weighed a half gram less than what other equivalent shoe, and yet, in a special test race through Death Valley, showed only 87 percent of the wear? What wacky brew of B-2s, B-6s, B-12s, measured out as precisely as the layers of colored dust on a butterfly's wing, could catalyze you into the original Uebermensch, pounding your pecs and yodeling as you knocked out personal best after personal best? If you didn't know it before, you knew it now, whether you wanted to or not . . .

The race began: we poured through the western edge of Manitou Springs, up a narrow gorge lined with houses, and up a pine-forested mountainside. Twenty minutes, approximately, and I was atop the first ridgeline, running with a string of six or seven others; many more racers up ahead, many more behind, strung out along the long trail. It was sunny and cool, exquisite running weather; the kind of a day that used to make me feel like I wanted to run forever, and could. Well, I didn't feel that way today: no desire, no fire, no leg.

American Indians used running as a deliberate way to power. There were no less than fifteen ritual footraces among the Hopis every year, each with its own divine purpose, its special and elaborate symbolic underpinnings: prayers, preparatory fasts, and abstinence from sex, powerful body paint and clothing. The Indians of Zuni Pueblo ran, kicking a three-inch sacred stick called a *tik-wa*, on twenty- to forty-mile circuits around their tribal fields, blessing the earth and crops with their will, their endurance. The Crows of the Northern Plains ran special footraces to earn good luck in hunting and war: to them, luck was not a matter of luck but something you could get, earn; the gods love gamblers, and they give out the mysterious substance to those who risk, push the limits.

This ritualization produced some incredible runners. Witness Wharton James's description of the running prowess of turn-of-the-century Hopis: "It is no uncommon thing for an Oraibi or Mishongnovi [two of the Hopi pueblos] to run from his home to Moenkopi, a distance of forty miles, over the hot blazing sands of a real American Sahara, there hoe his corn-field, and return to his home, within twenty-four hours. I once photographed, the morning after his return, an *old man* [italics mine] who had made this eighty-mile run, and he showed not the slightest trace of fatigue."

In 1979, Bernard Fontana hired an elderly Tarahumara Indian to carry a 65-pound earthenware jar out of a deep canyon in northern Mexico; the man lugged it out, sixteen miles, by night and was home again by dawn.

What did they have that I didn't have? I think I know, at

least part of it. A feeling of oneness with, closeness to, the world around them: running through, with, the landscape is a lot easier than running against it. Animism has its undeniable advantages: the same spirit flows through you and the country, and you can ride that idea as a surfer catches a wave—loose, unflexed, relaxed. I had felt some of that flow on those old runs back in Virginia, and to a lesser degree in the mountains above Telluride, but it was all gone now. I labored, panted, strained my way up the white giant's skin, feeling close to terrible and a million miles away from the nearest god.

It seemed strange to me, but people *talked* to each other while they ran; I am sure the real serious runners, the race leaders, didn't, but the main pack was amurmur with conversation. I met a California woman, Black Irish, eyes green as grass, from one of those California places that sound like El del San Huarache con Carne. She told everyone within earshot that she was in terrific shape and had run a 4:06 marathon a year ago and danced all night afterwards. Paul, from Boulder, was a glaciologist, a Gemini, and a mountaineer who had climbed Mount McKinley less than six months before. A lanky, long-limbed character, he looked like he could run up mountains with the best of them, but it wasn't so: "I pulled my right Achilles tendon last month," he said— runners love to *kvetch*—"and it's a miracle I can run at all. I'll probably have to have surgery." He didn't *look* like he needed surgery; a few minutes later he accelerated away, leaving the rest of the group in the dust. A fiftyish dentist, a ski patrolman from New Mexico . . . bits and pieces of a half-dozen biographies drifted into my ears. Even those people who didn't speak had their own ways of communicating: shirts. One unhappy-looking little man, with a white terrycloth headband and spotless white shorts and shirt—I called him "The Mahatma" in my mind—had written MARATHONS on his back, with a series of hash marks, like so: ⧸⧸⧸⧸ ⧸⧸⧸⧸ ⧸⧸. A sort of walking or running billboard for himself. Was one supposed to genuflect or merely applaud? I cannot recall all of the shirts, but a few were: *Phidippides, Feats Don't Fail Me Now, On the Run, Brooks* . . . Did I really see *Runners Do It Longer?* I hope not, but I'm afraid I did. I thought it all very, very strange; didn't people run to *escape* all of this? It seemed not. We carried our silliness with us even here, like spiritual steatopygia.

One hour, and into another . . . even the most long-winded socializers ran out of breath, fell silent. The trees thinned; up ahead, still far, far away, I could see the topmost rockpile of Pikes, high as two skyscrapers end on end. The leaders of the race, Chris Revelly and the rest (Trujillo had retired from competitive running, with a bum ankle—even the best of us can bite the dust*), were already up there, nearing the top. The scant dry air rasped in my throat, leaving a faint blood taste and a vast weariness in my calves and ankles. Have you ever fasted for a day and a half, two days, and felt the hunger grow in your belly till it swallows you whole? I felt that same kind of hunger now, for air, oxygen; I longed for the rich, oxygen-drenched vapors of sea level.

* For years Rick treated his chronic ankle tendon problems by soaking the sore extremity in ice water before going out to run; the cold deadened the pain. Eventually this hard treatment caught up with him: irreparable tissue damage.

The second hour went on and on, into the third. Runners began to pass now, going the other way, down; and I passed dropped-out racers in the screes, victims of altitude sickness, hypothermia (it was viciously chill in the wind), sprains, fatigue. I decided that I was going to quit when I got to the summit; *if* I got to the summit. I was burning out fast; my calves were about to croak. The California woman had pulled away from me and was a good mile ahead. My gait had faded from a slow lope into a creaky trot; I felt like an ancient, arthritic burglar trying to carry off a 300-pound wall safe on my back.

Two and a half hours (approximately): I collapsed on the alpine sod at an aid station and begged water and a couple of glucose tablets from one of the paramedics. Lay there, heart, banging against my rib cage like a panicked bird, nothing in my head but the odd bit of flying shrapnel: *all in . . . can't handle it . . . wasted . . .* Close to the ground, there was no wind; the sun warmed me. I imagined my bones dead, stripped of their aching flesh, slumbering on these tundras.

After five or ten minutes, I wobbled to my feet and headed on up the trail. "Go for it!" one of the paras called out, idiot slogan of hyper America. "Go for what?" I gurgled. What indeed?

The trail became even steeper; I had to use my hands in places to pull myself up over the boulders. The third hour was going fast, going, going, gone, and the field had thinned out. Most of the runners had finished, were about to finish, or had bagged it. At the top of the vast amphitheaters of smashed rock, against the sky, I could just make out the tattered line of spectators at the finish line. Was there really a finish line? It was somewhere up there, I supposed; still a long, long ways.

Into the fourth hour. Any thought of earning a vision or revelation was long gone by now; all I wanted to do was finish. I had a twenty-dollar bill wrapped in plastic in my sock; there was a snack bar at the summit, I knew, and I dreamed of the vulgarest kinds of food—greasy cheese-burgers, jelly doughnuts, soft drinks whose recipes read like Tocharian-B. Well, I would eat and drink them all when I got there. Meanwhile, I toiled up through the sunburnt slabs. Far below, behind, to the east, the brown summer plains rolled onto the curve of the planet itself; radiant toad-stools of cloud leaned against the edges of the sky. I had lost all real contact with my legs by now; they ran on their own, a drunken dance with hips that weaved, knees that knocked, and ankles that splayed. Out of control, and nothing I could really do about it but let them stumble on . . .

It took me three hours and fifty-eight minutes to get to the top; 735th, as it turned out, out of a thousand entrants, and just one second ahead of an eighty-five-year-old named Ivor L. Welch. Two minutes later and I would not even have been an official finisher. Twenty minutes below the summit, the Southern California woman had passed me, going down. She looked fresh as a new-minted penny and actually *laughed* as she went by: "If you're ever out in the L.A. area, look me up!" "Nevermore," I croaked, or something like that. My mind was too undone to manufacture sense, and my tongue too far gone to speak it.

For the first and only time in my life, I realized, I was both physically exhausted and mentally depressed. Almost always, when you wear your body down to the nub and come to the crux of the ordeal, the spirit soars. Not this time: quite the opposite. I felt let down, disappointed, cheated. The last of the magic from those old, lonesome runs in Virginia was gone; looking inside myself, I couldn't find the slightest trace of it. 14,110 feet up, I wandered aimlessly over the filthy summit screes, a loser.

It reminded me of the infamous Afghan Cobra and Mongoose Trick, which had been pulled on me on my last Asia trip. A street urchin marched up and down the sidewalk in Kabul—he looked like an Asian version of the old cartoon "Yellow Kid," in a dirty nightshirt and a skullcap—shouting "See cobra and mongoose fight! Fight to the death!" Behind him on the pavement were two large wicker baskets, containing the combatants. "Cobra, mongoose, fight to death!" A group of tourists and Westernized big-city Afghans gathered, and the boy collected money from them, tying it up in his shirt. "Cobra and Mongoose!" More people, more money . . .

Then suddenly, without warning, the boy bolted across the street, through the traffic, and was gone. The two baskets remained there on the sidewalk. After a few moments a tall, bearded Pathan leaned forward with his walking stick and tipped the baskets over. The lids fell off. No cobra, no mongoose. Empty.

I had forgotten something, something pretty obvious, in my obsession with biochemical processes: you could put together precisely the right physical conditions, but if the right mental or psychological or spiritual factors were missing, it was all for naught.

My running in Virginia and the early stages in the Rockies had inadvertently mimicked the mind-set that had preceded my Mount Neva climb: a peculiar kind of social isolation; a period of sexual near abstinence; an emptying out of my life, almost like the kind of emptying out shamans, yogis, lamas, and the rest do. Well, all of that was more important than I had thought, evidently. If I was going to push my game-playing out into that precious zone again, I would have to take the mind or spirit into account; it wasn't just an affair of the flesh.

8

My late-night visit with Dr. Andrew Weil was as extreme in its own way as my climbs, treks, and long-distance runs. I left New York City in a winter dusk, at rush hour from a Penn Station jammed with commuters, carrying a round-trip ticket to Amagansett, Weil's lair on the far tip of Long Island. The antique LIRR train bucketed and banged out through darkening Queens and on, at what seemed like thirteen miles per hour; the conductors looked and spoke like characters out of Beckett—"When do we get to East Egg?" "Depends on how fast the train gets there." "Is there any food on the train?" "Not unless you brought it with you." Dr. Weil picked me up at the pitch-dark Amagansett Station around nine o'clock; we talked at his house until after midnight, and sometime in the really bleak hours, the existential despair zone around three in the morning, I walked back to the station in a swirling snowstorm and caught the red-eye local back into the city.

Perhaps the lateness of the hour, the eeriness of the night hegira, added to the power of the meeting, just as bad weather, danger, and loneliness enhance the beauty and significance of a mountaintop. Easy things just aren't the same; they lose the sheen, the keen edge, "the fascination of what is difficult."

Whatever the reason, my meeting with Dr. Weil seemed to catalyze a whole spectrum of ideas that had been drifting, inchoate around inside my mind, especially my ideas concerning how the mind and brain function in stress situations. The meeting was a real turning point in my intellectual search for the mechanisms behind good and bad stress reactions.

"In looking at crises I've faced in my own past, I see a kind of pattern emerge," Weil said. "On the whole, my responses seem very predictable. There was something in my state of mind, in each case, that set me up for either a positive or negative performance."

He went on to tell of two cases in which he thought positively, with an almost implacable confidence, and everything worked out far better than it logically should have. In the first instance, Weil accompanied an ethnographer friend to a Yaqui Indian fiesta in Sonora, Mexico. Weil's friend had actually been trained as a Yaqui ritual dancer on previous visits with the tribe, and he ended up dancing with a different group than the one Weil was with. The Yaquis, of course, are the tribe that Carlos Castaneda made famous in the Don Juan books.

The mescal drinking and energetic dancing went on pretty much nonstop, far into the night; an exhausting routine for someone (like Weil) unused to it. Heat, dust, chanting,

stamping feet . . . To make things more intense, Weil was
the only non-Indian in the group, and he became the focus
of a lot of not entirely friendly attention: as he put it, "I
ended up interacting with a whole series of drunken, ag-
gressive Yaquis." Weil found that he could turn the Yaquis'
aggressiveness into friendliness in a matter of seconds—a
man would come over, ready to punch him, and ten seconds
later the two of them were joking and laughing like old
friends. Not only that: Weil's Spanish, usually a bit creaky,
flowed out smooth as silk, and he danced the unfamiliar
Yaqui ritual dance steps near perfectly. "I was feeling totally
nondefensive, just accepting everything that came at me,
and I found myself getting very high from the whole
process . . . I was definitely functioning on a supernormal
level."

Another time, when Dr. Weil was living near Tucson,
Arizona, some friends came visiting with a portable sweat
lodge. (Sweat lodges, important in Plains Indian ritual initiations, are structures about six feet across and four feet high
made of canvas or blankets over a framework of poles. You
build a big fire outside and heat stones till they are red hot;
avoid riverine sandstones and conglomerates, as they sometimes explode. You bring the hot rocks into the lodge with
a shovel, and pour water on them to make steam.) Weil and
company set up the lodge in a dry wash high in the mountains above Tucson, and did a really strong series of sweats.
Real sweating, by the way, is far from being a passive process.
When the steam reaches near unbearable temperatures, the
participants chant and sing loudly to mobilize their bodies
and minds in order to stand the stress. Sweating is specifically
a power-endowing process, in Plains Indian theology. When

they were done, Weil and one other person decided to run, barefoot, the two miles of rough canyon down to Weil's house. "Somehow I knew I was in a state where I couldn't make a mistake, couldn't get hurt," Weil recollected. "The feeling was that I wasn't thinking about where to put my feet; my consciousness was *in* my feet. I can't make that kind of thing happen at will, but something in the sweat lodge had set me up for it. My muscles and nerves and coordination, everything was working perfectly.

"If you repeat those kinds of acts and performances, you build up a kind of advance feeling about when you're going to do well and when you're not. Perhaps that's the first step in making your responses to stress better . . . There is power in doing the near impossible." Faith, in other words. "You have to have faith," Weil said. "It's a concept that really galls scientists, but in traditions like fire-walking or Mexican shamans dancing on sheer cliffs, faith is a prerequisite for having the experience."

What the sweat obviously did was to mobilize Weil's stress response equipment, the biochemicals and the rest, so that he was primed, ready, for the next stress situation he encountered, the headlong run down the canyon: almost like a vaccination, an inoculation of power-invoking stress. Faith mobilized by ritual ensured that the power would carry over. You chanted and prayed to the gods during the hottest, most unbearable part of the sweat, asking the supernatural powers-that-be to give you the strength and courage to withstand the heat. When the sweating is over, you still have the power the gods gave you, or at least the belief that the gods gave you power to sustain you in your next difficult situation. This seems to have been how the Plains

Indians, great believers in sweating, worked the process; and Dr. Weil's experience seems to have been constructed along those same general lines.

It takes faith, or something like it, to jump the gap; Weil gave as examples belief in gods (recall the Tibetan *tummo* adepts: they visualized the molecules of their skin transmogrified into thousands of powerful deities radiating heat), biofeedback (remember Joe Kamiya's alpha wave experiments), and placebos. Placebos are chemically inert pills given to patients with the advice that the pills are analgesics, muscle relaxants, stimulants—whatever effect the doctor wants to produce. In a surprisingly high percentage of cases, the pills produce the advertised effect, evidently by tricking— and triggering—the body's own endocrinal system into producing the appropriate chemicals. You have to have faith in the efficacy of the placebos for them to work.

"Faith can move mountains," or at least climb them. Shamans have known this fact and made use of it for millennia. In her marvelous 1923 anthropological monograph "The Guardian Spirit in North America," Ruth Benedict quotes the eighteenth-century historian Hockwelder: " 'The belief in these visions [sought deliberately through stress, under the tutelage of shamans] is universal among the Delaware Indians. I have spoken with several of their old men who had been highly distinguished for their valor, and asked them whether they ascribed their achievements to natural or supernatural causes, and they uniformly answered that, as they knew beforehand what they could do, they did it, of course.' " Benedict goes on to tell of how the Kootenay of the northern Great Plains threw themselves from the top of a tall tree, believing they could fly, or at least levitate their way to the ground safely; presumably some of them made it, though Benedict does not say so. She *does* tell of a Blackfoot medicine man, who leapt from a high cliff while in the transports of a vision, and survived.

The problem—there is always a problem, isn't there?—is what kind of faith?

Faith is dangerous stuff when taken straight, without a chaser; the blind kind can be downright deadly.

The kind of faith that works best is built on and tempered by experience, and the skill that comes from experience. You can bet that the Mexican *brujo* who danced on the cliff's edge, the Plains Indian medicine man who leapt from the tall tree, and the Nepali boy porter-*jangkri*, for that matter, who went head over heels down the snowfield didn't do these astonishing feats cold, they built up to them painstakingly, carefully, systematically, over long periods of time, and if the final act was in a sense a wild and thoughtless letting go of everything that had gone before, it was also only possible because they had so much to let go *of*. Recall, for instance, the parable of the frog in the milk.

The list of things that trigger altered states of consciousness is delightfully long; a partial catalogue, based on the works of Charles T. Tart and Marghanita Laski, reads something like this: solitary confinement; stimulus deprivation at sea, in the Arctic, the desert; highway hypnosis ("white line fever"); boredom; "kayak disease"—the disoriented dreamy state of Greenland Eskimos on long, lone voyages over empty waters; brainwashing and other third-degree interrogation techniques; contagious hysteria, as in mob scenes; orgies; panics; prolonged sentry duty or radar screen observation; fervent praying; intense absorption in a task or activity; meditation on a mantra or visualized deity or on one's own breathing; dehydration; fasting; insomnia; drugs; bad weather;

wilderness; sunrise, sunset; music; dance, both sacred and secular (dervishes, "breakers," et al.); exercise; desolation; light. Throw in Andrew Weil's list of ASC triggers—mango- and chili-eating, eclipses, the "whirl" dancing of children, and so on—and the list of triggers approaches comical proportions. Presumably one could flip into an altered state of consciousness by peddling an Exercycle in a dark room for twelve hours, or smoking six pipes full of strong tobacco on top of a three-day fast, or staring at the test-pattern mandala on the television set from two A.M. until six.

Any of these triggers probably has the potential to produce ecstatic mental states and supernormal physical performances. Most of the time they do not; on the contrary, their effects are usually downright destructive, physically and mentally. They may even cause visions and hallucinations that are life-threatening instead of lifesaving.

A couple of cases in point. The first case involves a group of sailors from a torpedoed British ship during the Second World War; their experiences were collected in an article entitled "Abnormal Mental States in Survivors, with Special Reference to Collective Hallucinations," by one Surgeon Lieutenant-Commander E. W. Anderson, in the *Journal of the Royal Naval Medical Service.* Anderson interviewed eleven of the survivors, men ranging from twenty to thirty-nine years in age; all had been on floats, half in and half out of the rough, icy waters (the torpedoing happened in June 1940, but the North Atlantic is always cold), for sixty-five hours or more before being rescued. They had no food or water during that time; most of their fellow sailors died in the torpedoing, drowned, or succumbed to exposure.

Anderson's findings were interesting for a number of

reasons. Several of the survivors shared common hallucinations, suggesting either that something like telepathy exists or that men share some deep mental substratum of ideas, concepts, and themes. Some of the common hallucinations can be ascribed to the power of suggestion—one individual "saw" something, and then persuaded those around him that they "saw" it, too—a process well know to all ad men, politicians, and propagandists, and not so remarkable. In other cases, however, men on floats far apart, unbeknownst to one another, shared visions. Some of these collective hallucinations were built around themes you might expect torpedoed sailors to draw on—rescue ships and planes, and shorelines, for instance—but others are not so easily accounted for. Why would two people independently dream up phantom dockyards or ghostly naval battles?

But the most important finding, in light of the quest I was on, was the almost total lack of *utility* of the visions; so far as the men's survival was concerned, their altered states of consciousness did nothing at all of significance, unless you count the man who saw a ghostly battleship and reported later that it "raised his spirits." They may as well not have had the visions at all, as far as survival was concerned. (It is a bit reminiscent of Winston Churchill's great nocturnal revelation. Churchill awoke in the middle of the night one night, convinced that he had just had a vision of the true meaning of all existence; half asleep, he scrawled it on a scrap of paper, only to awaken in the morning and read the following profound words: THE WHOLE IS PERVADED BY A STRONG SMELL OF TURPENTINE. Nonsense, dream junk.)

An even more instructive case, when considering the whole interrelationship between stress and altered states of consciousness, useful and otherwise, was the experience of the survivors of another torpedoed ship, a Dutch liner sunk in the South Atlantic on November 2, 1942. Three of the ship's crew, one American and two Dutchmen, endured eighty-three days together on a small raft before being picked up by a navy PC boat. During the first hours after the ship sank, Izzi, the young Italian-American, had a whole series of elaborate hallucinations; not only did they do nothing to save him but they nearly killed him. Izzi thought he was "going a mile a minute" on a motorboat captained by a silent Charon-like figure; then he was in the middle of a fleet, near "a big hole, where guys were going down for a cigarette"; then the torpedoed ship was resurrected from the deep, with men swimming over to it, the ship's cook serving them ham and eggs; a lunchroom, with coffee, hamburgers, doughnuts, pie. These scenes occurred over and over that first night, and again and again Izzi tried to swim away from the raft to reach the illusory food, drink, warmth, safety; if his friends hadn't restrained him, he would have swum away into the darkness and drowned. Indeed, two other men, Satterwhite and Autripp, fell victim to similar chimeras: Satterwhite saw a hill populated by friendly German spies with "plenty to eat," and told Autripp about it; the two men paddled away toward it and were never seen again.

Somewhere deep in the substrata of the mind and the brain, there is a place—it may be an actual anatomical zone, or it may not—where these mysterious responses (the visions, ecstasies, revelations, and the rest) are born.

One semi-plausible theory is Julian Jaynes', his idea of the bicameral mind. According to Jaynes, humankind was once possessed of a mystical, intuitive kind of consciousness, the kind we today would call "possessed"; modern consciousness as we know it simply did not exist. This prelogical mind was ruled by, and dwelled in, the right side of the brain, the side of the brain that is now subordinate. The two sides of the brain switched roles, the left becoming dominant, about three thousand years ago, according to Jaynes; he refers to the biblical passage (Genesis 3:5) in which the serpent promises Eve that "ye shall be as gods, knowing good and evil." Knowing good and evil killed the old radiantly innocent self; this old self reappears from time to time in the form of oracles, divine visitations, visions, etc.—see Muir, Lindbergh, etc.—but for the most part it is buried deep beneath the problem-solving, prosaic self of the brain's left hemisphere. Jaynes believes that if we could integrate the two, the "god-run" self of the right hemisphere and the linear self of the left, we would be truly superior beings. Perhaps that is what happens in these stress-induced interludes: a synergy of the analytical left side and the instinctual, empathic right—the golden mean of the skull's diaphanous tenant. It makes sense, whether it is exactly, literally true or not.

Another possible physiological locus for transcendent responses is that area of the brain mentioned earlier, the limbic layer, sometimes known as the reptilian brain, because it resembles structurally and functionally the brains of our premammalian ancestors. The limbic layer controls respiration, heartbeat, sleep, body temperature, blood pressure, and the like: all those functions which our everyday conscious mind cannot usually deal with at all without faith or placebos or some other trigger device as intermediary.

You would think that visions and other altered states of consciousness would spring from one of the more high-falutin, sophisticated parts of the brain, but a lot of man's most effective meditation techniques have focused on contacting the limbic layer. Zen, for instance: all of its abstraction and philosophizing really aim at nothing less than the death of all abstraction and philosophizing, and the resurrection of the simple animal self beneath. One basic form of Zen meditation simply consists of focusing one's attention on one's own breathing; put your mind into the rolling wheel of exhalation and inhalation, and ride it away . . . Zen also uses the *hara*, the part of the abdomen below the navel, as a meditation object; you sink your attention into it, out through the sub-basement door of the intellect, into the realm of, no pun intended, gut feelings, instincts.

Even Tibetan Buddhism, supposedly the most esoteric and complex offshoot of Buddha's teachings, is founded on this most basic biological bedrock. When I studied under Geshe Ngawang Darjay in India in the early seventies, the basis of the meditation practice I learned was following breaths, the same as in Zen: sit cross-legged, spine straight, hands in lap, and stick your mind on the infinite sea of gases flowing tidally in and out of your lungs. The Gelugpas were big on intellectual analysis—Nagarjuna, the great, scintillating philosopher of ancient India, is their kingpin—but again, they (and Nagarjuna himself) used the analysis to destroy all analysis, a self-destructing dialectic, everything blown away, nothing left but the immaculate, infinitely flexible self beneath it all.

"Buddha Nature," the Zen Buddhists call it; or "Big Mind," as opposed to the small mind we are trapped in, in our everyday lives. It sounds an awful lot like Jaynes' bicameral mind in action, or the limbic layer on the loose: what's in a name, anyway?

But still, why the good responses sometimes and the bad ones other times?

I think I know, and it has to do, again, with the power of faith and ritual.

The kinds of stress reactions you get in accidental situations, like torpedoings and shipwrecks, falls and lost waterholes and the rest, are catch as catch can. Maybe your body and mind just don't kick into stress response gear, or maybe they do, but you get a skewed physical response like too much adrenaline (as in my falling-rock incident) or a just plain weird and dysfunctional mental response like a nonsensical or even malign hallucination, the antithesis of Lindbergh's angels.

Practice, faith, and ritual push the odds way, way over onto your side. A sweat, for instance—you tell yourself that you need something like supernatural intervention or aid to make it through the heat; when you *do* make it through the heat, it is proof to you that that supernatural assistance did indeed arrive. Faith has sprung out of experience: and that faith, as Dr. Weil has pointed out, keeps open the channels between the conscious and the unconscious, between the everyday mind and the lost biochemical world within you.

I had unknowingly stumbled into a crude version of that process on Mount Neva, but I just hadn't pushed it through to its logical conclusion. I had built up tremendous faith in myself during my previous weeks of climbing, and added to it in the course of my long, hard walk into the mountain; and when I somehow survived that fall to the narrow ledge, it was the final message, telling me that I was tied in to some power far, far greater than myself. No wonder I climbed down the rest of the mountainside with such ease, such joyful grace: I was the gods' man.

Magic becomes a kind of habit after we do the difficult, the near impossible, over and over and over again; a habit that operates down in those oldest and deepest levels of the brain and the mind. Where pain and fear can be alchemized into blissful, sublime confidence, and stumblebums wake up to find themselves dancing on the business end of pins.

9

It was the spring of 1982; I was living back east, in the suburbs of Washington, D.C., again. Running to stay in shape, with an occasional tennis match now and then. A million leagues from those ecstatic days of running and climbing, so far back in my past. Thirty-eight years old and fading fast into Middle American torpor.

Late one night I found an old copy of *Mount Analogue* in a carton of books in my closet. Written in 1944 by the French climber/philosopher/poet René Daumal, *Analogue* is the story of a quixotic expedition to a mythical mountain on the shadow line between the physical and metaphysical worlds. The expedition is led by a guru figure named Sogol ("logos" backwards, of course), and includes such strange personnel as Russian linguist Ivan Lapse, American alpine painter Judith Pancake, and an Italian Hegelian tailor named Benito Cicoria (there are six others, equally fanciful: the tone of the book is a mixture of Tin Tin and Teilhard de Chardin). Anyhow, Sogol and his crew sail around the world in search of Analogue, break through a sort of fourth-dimensional wall, and find themselves at Port O'Monkeys, on the coastline beneath the flanks of the holy peak. To get to the top, they discover, they must become something more than human as they climb: the peak is like Nietzsche's bridge over the abyss to the next race beyond *Homo sapiens*. Its upper slopes are not of this world:

> There, on a summit more pointed than the finest needle,
> He who fills all space resides unto himself.
> On high in the most rarefied air where all freezes into
> stone,
> The supreme and immutable crystal alone subsists.
> Up there, exposed to the full fire of the firmament where
> all is consumed in flame,
> Subsists the perpetual incandescence.
> There, at the center of all creation, is he
> Who sees each thing accomplished in its beginning and its
> end.

Aided by the guides of Port O'Monkeys, Sogol's expedition climbs to Camp One, and there the book ends. Daumal died suddenly of tuberculosis; the book's last sentence, part of an extended essay on mountain ecology, trails off into endless silence: "Without the wasps, a large number of plants which play an important part in holding the terrain in place . . ."

Daumal's footprints led up through imaginary wastes of ice and snow, stamped like pagan psalms into that white desert. Someone had to follow, I thought; and that someone was me.

I really felt that I was ready to do something grand and magnificent in my search. I had figured out the map; now I had to go down the road.

I decided to try and climb Popocatépetl, "smoking mountain," the 17,887-foot volcano just south of Mexico City. It was big enough and remote enough to make climbing it a real project, a regular expedition, to be prepared for with almost ritual care. I liked that—it interrupted the secular flow of my life, broke it off. And as far as stress, visions, and the like were concerned, Popocatépetl was perfect terrain to search in. The great empty spaces of the mountain were a giant sensory deprivation/isolation chamber; and there was cold up there, and thin air, tent fever, risky ground—all the fine things that make high places so magical.

I would spend a week up there, alone, seeing what I could see; and then I would try and get to the summit if I could. From what I had heard of the peak, the standard route to the top was not difficult technically: steep, perhaps thirty-five degrees under the lip of the rim, but easy footing in the (usually) soft snow and loose volcanic turf. The difficulties sprang from the thin air, and the weather: white-outs in which mountaineers lost their way and fell to their death in the crater, or over the dazzling precipices to the southwest; ice storms that transformed the mountainsides into giant sliding boards of isinglass; driving sleet and freezing rain that soaked the finest gear through; that subtlest of assassins, hypothermia. Scores of people had died up there, over the years. The peak is a live one, too: the volcano erupted as recently as 1802, and present-day hikers and climbers frequently feel the ground tremble under them and smell sulfurous fumes on the air.

In the upper atmosphere, on those cold, extraterrestrial slopes, I would try out my ideas on isolation, stress, and the rest of it. My aim was not so much the physical summit of the volcano as some apogee of consciousness inside myself;

that's what I was climbing, working toward. With the out-
line of Analogue laid over the volcano, I would be climbing
physical and metaphysical peaks simultaneously, a holy
pilgrimage.

There is a peculiar joy to planning and putting together an
expedition, even the smallest, most quixotic one. One feels a
bit like the adventurous Belgian cartoon character TinTin,
setting off to search for the Abominable Snowman in Tibet,
or Donald Duck, preparing to travel to the desert and find
the Lost Dutchman Mine. It is a child's idea of what adult
life is supposed to be like, really: the daily training regimen
(five miles of running, a hundred sit-ups, two hundred push-
ups, all in a sweatsuit that makes you look like a Halloween
spaceman), the interminable equipment lists (twenty-four-
hour candles, underwater pens, Swiss army knives that can
do everything but sing the blues, big ruby antimalarial pills,
squeeze bottles of honey), the calendar with the days x-ed off,
one by one, approaching departure . . . It is how we should
live all the time—full of naiveté, innocence, a sense of profound, playful importance—and almost never do.

So it was with Popocatépetl. I began preparing for the
trip the day after I decided to go, late in May: booking
tickets (leaving July 28th), saving money, trying to work
myself into shape for the high altitudes. I felt a surge of
purpose, an ecstatic kind of acceleration: eight weeks before
I was due to leave, and the fact of it pinned everything up
taut, fine. There was no loose time all of a sudden: the rhythms of my existence rolled together, coalescing toward the
great volcano. I bought an ice ax and a new pair of heavy
mountaineering boots; I got a Mexican Tourist Card at the
shabby little consular office on 16th Street in Washington.

I ran 38, 45, 53, 62 minutes a day, grinding out the miles. It is amazing how quickly one's physical condition deteriorates through hypokinesis (underuse), on the wrong side of thirty-five. Staying in halfway decent shape is a constant struggle with a constant, nagging sense of hopelessness, as if one were polishing brasswork on the *Titanic*.

By July 28th, my jumping-off date, I was at least vaguely in shape and had my gear assembled: it weighed in at just over fifty pounds. The only thing I didn't have was a proper camp stove. My old one turned out at the last minute to be broken, and I had spent too much money outfitting the trip to buy a new one. I settled on twenty solid-fuel canisters, cakes of Sterno-like stuff, the kind bums use to cook mulligan stew by the railroad tracks. I liked the fact I didn't have a proper stove, actually; it was a kind of gesture against the equipment mania that possesses so many climbers, especially Americans these days. Who really cares about fancier and trickier gear after a while? Too many people; and they lose sight of the game itself, and the peculiar relationship between man and mountain.

Climbing has always been split into two opposing schools: a mainstream obsessed with technology, egomania, and careerism, and a splinter group of mystics and crazies. Maurice Wilson of course fell into the latter category (no pun intended). And Hermann Buhl, the Austrian alpinist who used to bicycle alone up into the Tyrol on weekends to climb, ropes and iron on his back. Once, cycling home at night, he fell asleep at the handlebars and woke up with his bike and climbing gear in the icy waters of a mountain river. Buhl climbed to the summit of Nanga Parbat alone when his climbing partner got sick at the highest camp; climbed continuously for thirty-six hours, staying awake on Dexedrine.

Photographs of him when he staggered back down to meet the rest of the expedition show a face burned away to a gaunt dervish's, ghostly, haunted, mad. Buhl later died on Chogolisa ("Bride Peak") when a giant cornice gave way beneath him. And there were certain climbers in Boulder, Colorado, back in the sixties who did their climbs in secret, in bad weather or dead of night: others found their footprints in the snow, ending at the base of impossible walls, or discovered their pitons in high fissures where no one had gone before.

It was a nice ideal; it was, I thought, what climbing was all about.

I rode out to Dulles Airport with my overloaded Lowe Pack; I had so much gear I had to lash my tent, in its stuff sack, on the outside. I caught a plane to Houston, laid over there a few hours, and then caught Pan Am's red-eye flight south to Mexico City. We landed sometime after one in the morning, late, and I didn't get to my hotel till after two. It had been raining, and the air was cool and musty and bittersweet with coal smoke; and hard to breathe, at over six thousand feet above sea level. I slept half the next day, and the day after, around noon, I got a ride up to the volcano, an hour and a half away. Sprawling slums, high plateau, then a steep climb through cloudy forests . . . The huge chalet at Tlamacas, on the saddle between Popocatépetl and its sister peak, Iztaccíhuatl (17,343 feet), was virtually deserted; summer is the bad weather season on the volcanoes, and few people go there then. I paid off my driver, filled my water bottles in the chalet rest room, and lugged my pack up the first slopes. Popo looked enormous, looming above: snaggly ridgelines, rust-colored cliffs, dustings of snow, bulging domes of antediluvian ice, sinister fissures and crevasses . . . Fire and ice had happened here, an awful lot of both. I thought of Aztec gods, tombs, witch doctors and curses: it was that kind of place.

That first day on Popocatépetl, I hiked up a hundred yards or so above Tlamacas, into the fields of volcanic dust, and set up camp. At midafternoon it was already dark as dusk: the rusty cone, with its tilted skullcap of ancient ice, disappeared in cloud; mists rose through the forested valleys below. I felt disoriented and strange, stranger than strange, from the 13,000-foot jump in altitude, the jump in place, Washington to Texas to Mexico City, to a burned-out cinder pile at the edge of nowhere.

I dumped the contents of my pack out on the ground, took the tent out of its stuff sack, and stamped out a level place to pitch it on. Using my ice ax as a mallet, I drove the aluminum pegs deep into the loose ashen ground; it didn't feel completely secure, far from it, but you can only do what you can do. I excavated a small pit just outside the tent door, placed one of the fuel cans at the bottom, and set it ablaze with a match; poured a couple of inches of water into the cookpot, and balanced it over the silky blue flame. 6:33, the digits on my watch said. Leopards chased their tails in my skull. The clouds had closed in; visibility was down to no more than thirty feet at the most. I emptied two packets of freeze-dried food, chop suey and meatballs, into the pot. Voices drifted up from the trail below, Mexicans hiking back down to Tlamacas.

By 7:15 it was sleeting against the sides of the tent; the air was cold, and my exhalations made silver plumes. I ate the improvised stew as soon as it was warm, and some de-hydrated pineapple, chunks as light as cork, excruciatingly sweet. The rain came in harder, roaring across the mountainside. When I peered out, just before falling asleep, I saw tiny white dots bouncing on the black ground. I reached out my hand, and brought back beads of ice, dead white: snow.

When I awoke the next morning, at just past six, the storm had blown itself out. Except for a lid of strangely scalloped cloud on the summit, Popo was crystal clear. There was fresh snow on the glaciers and a dusting down the rock ridges, but where I was camped it had mysteriously vanished, melted and evaporated away on the bone-dry lava soil.

I ate a tiny breakfast—a fragment of chocolate, a couple of cups of water—and broke camp by sunrise. I didn't have far to go that day: I planned to hike to the Las Cruces Hut, where the real steep climbing begins—two or three hours away, I thought.

The compass rose in my mind's eye must have withered away in the night, because the first thing I did was take the wrong turn in the trail, up a horrid slope of mushy scree to a nameless ridge under Popocatépetl's southwest corner. Totally inexplicable. The way to Las Cruces is absolutely obvious, impossible to miss; but I had done so. I had to backtrack, across more sliding wastes of igneous shrapnel, to pick up the trail. An hour wasted in all, and I had the depressing feeling you get when you burn up a lot of energy for nothing. It was a queerly put together day, too, lit like a bad print of an early Ingmar Bergman film, stark and dark. I stopped frequently to rest on the trail; passed two or three people, Mexican hikers: "*Buenos días.*" I was too tired to try and speak Spanish; I tried to smile, and pointed up toward the summit vaguely: "*Mañana.*" They must have thought me an idiot.

I crossed a ravine between twisted basalt cliffs, the rocks

covered with the kind of spray-painted graffiti you see in New York City subway cars, ROCK Y BLUES, CLUB ALPINISMO MONTERREY, dozens of names, even an improvised advertisement for some local brand of mountain tent. There was no water in the ravine bottom, nothing but empty cans and wrappers. After the ravine, I passed more ghastly, tilted dunes of lava gravel. On and on they went, up and up, a landscape of splendid ugliness.

I did the last grind up to the Las Cruces hut just after noon, staggering up through the middens of trash left by decades of climbers and hikers: beer cans, *jugo* cartons, plastic, streamers of toilet paper—an archaeology of Mexican recreation. Las Cruces took its grim name from the three or four corroded man-sized crosses propped in the screes behind the hut, in memory of the dozens of climbers who have died on the peak. The hut itself, a sawed-off quonset hut on a concrete base, looked like it had been bombed: the whole front was missing, torn away. An avalanche? Vandals? Impossible to say, but I suspected the latter. More heaps of garbage stirred in the wind. A charming scene, all in all.

I had found no water on my way up from Tlamacas, not a drop: my water bottle was empty, and my throat ached with thirst. I found a hummock of old snow, filthy with lava dust, in the shade of the hut's eastern wall: nasty stuff, indeed, but it looked like a cache of ambrosia to me. I stuffed my mouth with the black stuff and filled the cookpot, fired up a can of fuel and set the pot on it to make water. It was early, but I decided to camp to catch my physical and mental breath; I was beat. I dumped my tent out on the ground, stomped the stakes into the loose turf, snapped the aluminum poles together. The altitude and my general tiredness made the job harder than it should have been; it took me nearly half an hour to get it done, the end ropes fastened to big chunks of basalt, everything secured.

Rain began to fall; clouds rode in out of the east on the wind. The seas brewed these storms and sent them across intervening land to crash against Popocatépetl; it could get bad, especially in midsummer. I half remembered talking to a Mexican climber once, in an airport somewhere, a tall, crop-skulled, cornflower-blue-eyed Teutonic Mexican who said, "Once, I think it was your June, five students, three boys and two girls, went climbing on the peak. It was warm, and there were just a few clouds. They climbed up above Las Cruces, all the way to the summit—there was almost no snow that year, and it was easy. Then without warning the weather closed in. Visibility was under twenty feet, and freezing rain coated the rocks. They had ice axes but no crampons, no rope, and light clothing. They tried to descend but lost their way, and ended up on the cliffs to the south of the usual route. One woman slipped and fell, and they saw her vanish into the clouds below. The other woman lost her nerve and clung to the rocks—she refused to move. The others finally had to leave her there. One man died on the way down, fell, and a second collapsed just above the Las Cruces hut, and died of exposure there. The other man, the last one, made it down to Tlamacas and died after telling his story." It sounded like a tall one, a yarn, but who could say?

Meanwhile the rain turned to snow, grapnel, slung like bullets on the wind. The tent ropes hummed, the fabric of the roof cracked and snapped. I had a terrible headache and no energy at all. I wrote in my journal for a while, recording the nonevents of the day, and then I just lay there, my head propped against my pack. It was hard to relax, with the weather so busy outside; I kept waiting for a seam to pop, a fiberglass pole to snap, the whole damned thing to collapse. Some of the gusts must have been fifty, sixty, seventy miles an hour, and the tent was old, its fabric brittle. I managed to pull the cookpot inside, but I couldn't bring myself to drink more than a mouthful of the ashen water.

As the afternoon began to ebb, I managed to rouse myself enough to go outside and check the tent stakes, to make sure they were holding. Remarkably, everything seemed secure; the snow, or whatever it was, was still coming in from the northeast, but the wind hadn't worsened. I went back inside, added some instant coffee to the dingy snowmelt in the pot, and washed down four quarter-grain tablets of Mexican codeine. A half hour later the iron mask of headache began to lift off my face; I felt almost good.

The codeine was probably a mistake, a stick in the biochemical spokes, but what could I do? My head felt like it was going to crack, my face was twisted with cramp, nausea roiled in my belly . . . It was either the codeine or chuck the whole thing, descend to a lower altitude, give up.

The problem with taking the stuff was it flew right in the face of the whole idea of the stress-into-bliss power equation. Just in crass physical terms, codeine occupied the same receptor sites as endorphin, which meant the whole endogenous painkilling system was short-circuited . . . And in theological or spiritual terms, it was as if I were trying to cheat the gods—they traded visions and powers only for real, unadulterated hardship, not for second-rate buffered stuff. I imagined a Plains Indian bringing a Walkman on a vision quest to keep from getting lonely, or Buddha sitting on an Ensolite pad beneath the Bo-tree . . . No, it was ridiculous.

But again, what could I do? And the stuff *did* work, no

doubt about it. A half hour after I took the codeine, the pain dissolved away; an hour or so later, sleep crept over my weary body and mind.

When I awoke, around nine, most of the clouds had blown out; the wind still whipsawed across the lava deserts. A half moon had risen, illuminating the sky, the mountain. I ate a packet of freeze-dried pears, and drank a few more swallows of owl juice. Lying there in my sleeping bag, I laid out plans for the next days: move camp up to the snowline, the nearest source of water; load up on liquids and try to eat; recharge myself. Today's headache and confusion and weakness were all signs of AMS, acute mountain sickness, thin air aggravated by dehydration: bad, especially when you are alone.

And what of my grand reasons for coming here? Well, I had no idea whether I would find anything or not. Nothing was clear. If Nirvana was about to pounce out of those clouds of unknowing, it was news to me. What did I know? Nothing, *nada*. See your own skeleton; place a drop of curare on your tongue and whisper *abracadabra* with your last breath; fill your pockets with stones and leap ass over teakettle into the Void. Foolishness to the nth power.

Cold, gloom: I pressed the button on my watch and tiny, apocalyptic numbers appeared in the dark: 5:58 in fire. My head throbbed and my mouth was gritty with volcanic dust. I had a vague recollection of too many dreams—disturbing pieces of pictures, of crowded buses, wintry cities, roads to nowhere—images that slipped away before I could catch them. Dream junk, again.

It had snowed enough the night before to build up a good inch of slush on the east side of the tent. I put on boots and mitts, went out with the cookpot, scraped enough snow to fill it, lit another fuel can. A long, long time later, I had enough melt for half a cup of lemonade. I drank it and went back outside. The mountainside was absolutely still: the sound of one hand clapping, a silence that rang with unborn sound. There was no wind at all. Clouds drifted up from below. Six or seven hundred feet below, the highest tussocks of grass, pallid tassles that looked far more dead than alive, vanished in the mist. Two ravens, Mexican edition of *Corvus corax*, rose from the refuse heaps below the hut and flapped away. I was the only living thing left.

By 8:30 I was packed up and moving. Slowly, incredibly slowly.

The primordial iron landscape stretched away, up into the hanging mists, steeper and steeper as it rose, hopelessly vast and desperately unlovely in the brooding flat-light. I thought of the juggernaut crushing people beneath its giant wheels. With every step I sank into the loose stuff of the mountain, dragged my foot out, and set it down again. This wasn't mountaineering as I had known it in the past, in the Rockies and the Himalayas, on hard, faceted stone, diamond snow. I was stumbling and swimming in gormless murk, like Peer Gynt in the Boyg's coils.

My weariness depressed me; my depression wearied me. It shouldn't have been as hard as it was, but it was; it got worse the further I went. I had to plan out every move and string them together like beads to keep going. Trudge up to that yellow chunk of pumice, collapse to my knees; crouch there, heart pounding, head splitting, for exactly two minutes, rationing out the rest time on my watch; then up again, and on, fifteen, twenty, twenty-five steps, and another collapse.

One step, four breaths; one step, six breaths. Somewhere up there, there is snow, I told myself, where I can slake this murderous thirst. Somewhere up there, I can stop and rest.

It took me until just after 1:00 P.M. to find a spot to bivouac: a minuscule flattish place, an indentation in the vast and dreary slope, with a dirty little snowfield twenty feet away. I spent most of the next half hour building up the edges of the niche with rubble, trying to build enough of a platform to support the tent properly. I succeeded: it was a shabby, half-assed job of riprapping, but it would just have to do. I used the biggest rocks I could find to anchor the guy lines that held down the tent's two ends: the wind was coming up again, and I was really afraid the whole contraption, with me in it, might bolt over the edge and down the rockslides in the night.

When I was through, I had a pretty fair campsite, all things considered. My front door looked up into a charnel house of gray dust, exploded rock bombs, and patches of snow, clouds pouring across it like smoke from a burning world. Out the back door, nothing but space: nothing.

I filled my cookpot at the snowfield, a messy amalgam of dead snow, ice, lava gravel. It occurred to me that I hadn't really eaten in over thirty-six hours; perhaps that helped explain my lassitude. Hauling sixty pounds on your back, at 15,500 feet, up the world's gloomiest rockfields, with nothing but thin air in your belly: that could burn anybody out. I lit a fire just outside the tent door; it took forty minutes to make two inches of hot water. I added two freeze-dried dinners, meatballs and chop suey, mashed them into an edible goo, and ate all of it, followed by bread and chocolate.

There was lots of weather that afternoon. Thunder rolled

in the dark cloudbanks below the peak. The clouds rose; by five it was snowing again, flakes sailing like sparks over the screes, drumming against the walls. Grapnel, then wet powder: within half an hour the whole mountainside was white, as far as the eye could see, and still it snowed.

I fell asleep; when I woke, the tent was full of refracted moonlight. I put my parka on and went outside. Below, a sea of clouds covered the world, gray; a faint erubescence far, far to the west marked the grave of the sun. It looked like you could walk out onto those clouds and walk away forever. Only the great pinnacle of Ixtaccihuatl confronted Popocatépetl, across fifteen miles of thin air. The snows around my camp shone like steel; frost crystals glinted here and there. The moon was just a shave off full.

Across the planet, how many people were as high as I was? There were a few thousand Quechua Indians, tin miners, potato farmers, coca-leaf caravaneers, in the Andes, riprap huts and shacktowns scraping the stars. Yak herders camped out on the Ch'ang T'ang of Tibet; the outcast Bhot hunter, with his carbine and wolf-dog, crossing a 20,000-foot icefield. Hindu saddhus listened to their beards grow in the peaks behind Dharmsala. Climbers bivouacked on Denali, Huascarán, Tirich Mir . . . A cosmonaut slept in the radiant vacuum over Australia.

There is a certain feeling, at high altitudes; you even get a touch of it in the artificial atmosphere of an airplane cabin. You are out on the edge of the human world; even as you long for the warmth, the noise, the comfort and reassurance of that world, something else draws you farther out, into the unknown. The cash and credit cards in your pocket will not help you. All the old bets are off . . .

Looking down the white slopes, I saw no one, nothing: a world clean as a gnawed bone, pure, dead.

Dawn came like a tremendous fire pushed up from underground. 5:45; another brutal headache gripped me between the eyes. I drank down the last of the lemonade, with three codeine tablets.

Lying there in my sleeping bag, watching the daylight grow stronger, I experienced the same feeling of extreme isolation, of being far out on the edge of things, that I had felt the night before. At the same time I felt as if I were on the verge of discovering something: as if, in going to the outermost limits of my known world, I were in the position to sight an entirely new continent of consciousness. It was out there, I felt, like the New World in 1491, known only through strange deviations in the currents and winds.

Again, it must have been the altitude, compounded by the loneliness, the austere conditions: just as I had planned. The mind manufactures things, squeezes them out of literal thin air: a feeling of impending light, of Godhead about to croak a message. The mountains, I have found, are perfect country for this. In a 360-degree tabula rasa of snow, rock, ice, and sky, the mind's eye is driven to search for significance, signs. A dark rock has collected enough solar heat to gnaw through a foot of snowpack. Crow tracks in glacial flour end in midstride, leapt into space. A single cloud the size of a pocket handkerchief strikes the moon and incinerates. It all seems to have profound meaning, as if whole empires, worlds, rode on these obtuse phenomena. They are the stuff gods and goddesses are made of.

I wasn't going anywhere today, just too worn down; a good thing, since I was still totally wasted from the last two days. It took me twenty minutes to put on my cap, gloves, boots; I moved like a deep-sea diver in a dream, a sleepwalker. So much for clicking into superior performances, I thought, and managed to laugh. A chilly, windy day outside. I scooped up more snow with my mittens and tried to light another fuel can. It took a whole book of matches, because of the dampness, the sullen heaviness of the air. "For want of a nail, a shoe was lost," etcetera; more mountaineers have probably been slain by fires that wouldn't catch than by falls: can't get warm, can't melt water, can't eat, can't see . . . dead. When a flame finally appeared, it seemed as unreal as the spirit coaxed from a Ouija board.

The clouds boiled up from the lower slopes. The top of the mountain was bathed in a fine silver light. It was very cold.

I felt close, so close, all that long day.

I woke at 3:45 A.M. with another headache and a bastard of a sore throat. The air was even danker than before, if that was possible; it smelled of sulfur, from the crater above. When I looked outside, utter misery: nothing but clouds roiling and snaking over gray snow and rock debris. *Tomorrow*, I said to myself, *you had better climb that last two thousand vertical feet of mountain. Because if you don't, you never will.* My energy and enthusiasm were running out fast.

I lit the candle, a tremendous light. Took two codeines, and then two more. Was my trip collapsing around me? I wasn't sure, and I wasn't sure I cared, either. I was physically and spiritually dog-tired.

At 5:45 there was still no sun, but the clouds were beginning to grow more distinct and at the same time thinner.

I could see a good half mile up the mountainside, up dizzying no-man's-lands.

According to Hultgren's definitive article "High-Altitude Medical Problems" in the July 1979 *Western Journal of Medicine*, the thin air of high altitudes automatically brings about a condition called hypoxia, which is simply the lowering of the oxygen levels in the arterial blood. At sea level, oxygen levels may exceed 90 percent; at high altitude, after heavy exertion, they may plummet to under 40. Effects of hypoxia include headaches, lassitude, malaise, insomnia, strange dreams, and hallucinations. That was what was happening to me, I thought. My fingers felt like someone else's chopsticks. Thin air, thick blood . . . and bad dreams swimming upstream to spawn.

There comes a point in every adventure when you have to ask yourself, *What the hell am I doing here?* The cold (or heat or sun or aridity: name your misery) has worn you down to a kinked frazzle; you are sick of the bad food and the foul water, of sleeping with a bent neck and a twisted spine. Your clothes smell like harvest time on the mildew farm. Boredom fastens on your throat like a vampire. The summit or lost city or headwaters of the sacred river or Great McGuffin—whatever it was you set out to find—suddenly loses all credibility; even if it is there, and you get it, who cares?

That was how I felt as the day bored on into late afternoon, and the snows rotted away on the scabrous cinder fields. I wished I could have packed up the whole thing, wind, dark, cold, the works, wrapped it up in brown paper and mailed it to the opposite end of the earth. I wished I were sitting in a café on the Avenida Reforma, listening to Mexican rock on the jukebox, with one of those thin Chihuahua steaks smothered in violent green chili in front of me, and a tall bottle of Carta Blanca . . . Or lying on a beach, with the Pacific swells rolling in . . . Anyplace but this gigantic nullity, this tomb of black fires.

And so the wasted day turned to wasted night.

At 5:42 A.M., when I came to, the night was still glowing. I washed down a bone sandwich with a cup of dust; stuffed my pack full of every piece of loose gear I could find, for the weight—remember, hardship was what I was looking for—donned my boots, gloves, and parka, slung the pack on my back, and crawled out into the frosty light. Noctilucent clouds drifted like levitated ingots of gold overhead.

The snows were all gone from the mountainside. Gravel, dust, and depth hoar crunched under my boots. The thin gases blazed in my lungs. You call this stuff air? I felt dizzy, dry, and weak. The only way I was going to make it to the summit, I realized, was to keep the idea of climbing in the center of my mind, and wind the mainspring of my will around it tight. Questioning was a luxury I could not afford; monomania was the order of the day.

The sunrise struck a half hour after I began climbing. One moment the cumulus cloudbanks below were as dark and cold-looking as icebergs; the next, as if a switch had been flicked somewhere, they began to glow, violet, viridian, then amber. Within a few minutes the whole northwest side of the volcano stood revealed; I could see all the way to the skyline, where a thin rampart of snow shone, pale salmon in the dawn. The rocks, drused in red light, might have been plucked from a photograph of the surface of Mars.

The higher I climbed, the steeper the terrain became; I needed my ice ax to hold on, driving the shaft deep into the plutonic detritus.

On and on, up and up; I came at last to the snowfield: bad stuff, the consistency of damp sugar, with ice underneath. I kicked steps in it, a ladder of them, a hundred feet, two hundred . . . Crampons would have been nice. My boots skidded, an ominous sashay on the ice; one bad slip, I thought, and I will be gone.

Up and up . . . and then suddenly the sky was whizzing past my ear like a scythe; I crawled up on my hands and knees, till I was staring down into the blind skull's eye of the crater.

I felt that same sense of bliss, a joy beyond comprehension, that I had felt on Mount Neva; a feeling that all ills were healed, everything was all right, always had been, really, and always would be. There was nothing wanting in all of creation; anything less than perfection was impossible, it just couldn't happen. I felt this in every fiber of my being, every cell in my body.

There was something missing, however; I searched for it, but it just wasn't there. The physical powers, the boundless strength, the Nijinskian sense of balance: I had had it all on Neva, but it wasn't here now. On the contrary: I was all in, kaput. My legs wouldn't support me; I sank to my knees, and bowed over till my forehead was pressing into the snow.

The mountain, and the week of little food, isolation, altitude, jet lag, and whatever else, had done me in: handed me my rear end on a platter. I wasn't going to be taking any Herculean steps today, no way. Was it the codeine, shorting out the biochemical circuits? Or were the gods just not in a giving mood that day? I couldn't tell; but in another sense I didn't really care. The bliss poured through my wrung-out flesh and tired bones; the rest of it I would get another time. I knew that for a fact.

What did I bring back from Popocatépetl? Two small, withered pebbles of pumice plucked from the sodden ashes as I descended in the rain. A half-dozen postcards ("¡Postales Tarjetas!") of the mountain, shot at dawn from the air, the frozen roan cone soaring into a fluorescent green sky. Two ounces of ebony sand (approximately) that spilled from my boots and sleeping bag when I unpacked in my hotel room in the little town of Amecameca that night. That was all.

But I had really come close, I felt; I had touched something, contacted something extraordinary, not of this world. Again: Neva, those lone runs in Virginia, and now this. Another day up there, perhaps, sitting in the cold darkness of the tent . . . What was it Kafka wrote?

You do not need to leave your room. Remain sitting at your table and listen. Do not even listen, simply wait. Do not even wait, be quite still and solitary. The world will freely offer itself to you and be unmasked, it has no choice, it will roll in ecstasy at your feet.

I don't know; I think it helps if your room is a tent seventeen or eighteen thousand feet in the air on a frozen mountain . . . But the principle is the same. I had grazed the Light, up there; if I had given it a little more time, the world would have rolled for me, I was sure; I would have gotten my song. And I would yet.

10

Still living back east, in the suburbs of Washington, D.C., I continue on with my quest. A weird place to vision-hunt, perhaps, but also appropriate—I mean, if these games really contain the means to personal power, they should work anywhere there is isolation, risk, hardship. A patch of Virginia hardwood forest between the highways and the river, as well as the High Himalaya or the eastern California desert or midocean.

What I know now: it is very, very simple, and there are no tricks, really. Play the game by your lonesome. On short rations, as hard as you can, and if you keep your mind on the search and your eyes open, you will eventually find it. And after you've found it once, twice, and again, it will begin to stick—the power and the bliss will work itself into the grain of your life, changing everything. It is true, and that's that.

On a cold winter day in 1984 I set out on one of these strange things I call "woods runs." Out across a certain tract of hardwoods I know of, on the cliffs overlooking the

Potomac River's fall-line. A grim, gray landscape today, ice in the water, leafless trees like castles of dead sticks, the owl-dark ground frozen hard as rock. Mad dogs and Englishmen go out in the noonday sun, but this is much, much better: a sunless February, an inchoate chunk of aboriginal East, and nowhere in particular to go. Perfect.

Woods runs are something like Rick Trujillo's H,T&E runs through the mountains, and something like a game sometimes played by climbers in the eastern Sierra Nevada called "Nothing Can Stop Me." "NCSM" goes like this: you straight-edge a line across a U.S. Geological Survey relief map and then you follow it across the actual landscape, no matter where it goes, swimming rivers and lakes, climbing cliffs, bushwhacking maquis and gulches, etc. The only real rules are laid down by the terrain itself, the lay of the land (and water), angle and pitch, gravity and the rest.

Lois Fischer, a Bishop, California, climber, skier, kayaker, and what have you, explains: "It started out by accident, really, on the approaches to climbs. We would be up some-place like Big Pine Canyon, in the Palisades, and someone would look at the map and discover a shortcut off the trail to wherever we were going to climb. In Big Pine, you started out traversing a steep, steep manzanita slope, a half hour of sheer torture, and then you crossed south-facing scree slopes, over dry talus, with lush little springs here and there, and tiny wildflower gardens. Then you came to steep cliffs and outcroppings only a couple of hundred feet high but really challenging and fun to cross; and after that, big granite blocks you crawled over, under, and through. At first we did it just to save time, but then people began to discover how much fun it was. Climbing guides from the Palisades School of Mountaineering would go up for a whole half day or day of it, just traveling across the roughest sections they could find."

Tom Carter and Allen Bard evolved their own variant out of eccentric ascents they began to do in Yosemite a few years back as an escape from the highly competitive rock-climbing scene there, with its egomaniacal careerism and frantic reputation-building. They did what they called "mungey climbs," abstruse, obtuse routes up ridiculous geological features, things like conglomerate-and-mud walls, hanging brush fields, and cliffs so decadent you could sneeze holes in the rock; they used dog screws, those long lanks of iron that police dogs and Dobermans are tethered to, for pitons. When they weren't mungey climbing (the word *mungey*, incidentally, denotes trash, garbage; it derives from *muck* and *grunge*), they put up ascents on normal rock-climbing routes in foul weather, climbed the gigantic wall of Half Dome by moonlight, etc. In recent years, the Bard-Carter team inaugurated what they call "red-line traverses," in which they pick a contour (altitude) line on a survey map and follow it as it unravels. They pick, of course, the nastiest lines, looping around ridgelines, across glaciers (on skis), over unknown and extremely difficult cols, all high above timber limit; some of their journeys last for days and days, often in the dead of winter.

Why, you may ask, do these games have a peculiarly magical quality, while even more strenuous sporting events, such as the Hawaii Iron Man Triathlon, the Western States 100, and TV's *Survival of the Fittest* competition,* do not?

---

* The Iron Man consists of a 2.4-mile open-sea swim, a 112-mile bicycle ride, and a 26.2-mile marathon laid end to end without a break. The Western States 100 is a 100-mile footrace over the

The reason is this, in my opinion: the latter are all group, competitive, organized affairs, ego against ego, winner and loser—pure poison if one is looking for something mysterious and powerful to come out of one's games. Even worse, both the Iron Man and *Survival* are highly commercialized to boot, with big prize money, advertisers, and sponsors, the same joyless carapace that has stifled so many other fine games; and the antithesis of the existential passion that propels, H, T&E runs mungey climbs, woods runs, and whatever other covert games are being played out there in the bush by the true believers. Playing games to win has very little if anything to do with the mad and holy act that lies at the heart of the matter. It's all right if that's what you want to do, but it's not where the real magic is.

So off I go, this darkling day, down the hard trail through the dreary woods. A flat stretch, and then a loop up across a patch of bog, fallen trees and ponds full of splintered ice; then up the flanks of a ridgeline and along the crest and down again, following a skein of trails memorized from the map; and then off the trail, down into a bowl with a mummified stream at the bottom, shoes snapping the frosted leaves on the ground like shards of parchment; up a steep knoll, and down the other side.

Even without leaf the trees are thick enough to make navigation difficult; I don't really know if I'm going west, south, or someplace in between. The creeks are no help;

Sierra, with 17,010 feet of altitude gain, 21,970 of altitude loss, and temperatures ranging from freezing to 100 plus. *Survival of the Fittest* encompasses wilderness running, floating whitewater in life jackets, free rappeling, aerial obstacle courses, even Robin Hood-versus-Little John-style stick fighting on narrow bridges.

they coil around aimlessly in the muddled topography of the forest floor . . . But it doesn't matter, I'm not going anywhere in particular anyway.

In a woods run, like H,T&E, but unlike "Nothing Can Stop Me," you run whatever line pleases you—in circles if you want—through the wilds. The only general rule is you don't avoid obstacles; you go, whenever at all possible, over and through them. With relish, squeezing every last bit of challenge out of the land.

After a while I come to the gorge cut by Difficult Creek, descend the steep slopes down to the creek bottom, and turn east toward the river. I have only been running about half an hour, the real bushwhacking and climbing are still to come, and already I am winded. "When you go looking for God, be sure and pack a lunch," someone once said; several, in fact. The search goes on and on ad infinitum, ad nauseam: the insane in pursuit of the incomprehensible across the impassable . . . to the limit and beyond.

In a fascinating little essay entitled "Border Tribes," published in *Coevolution Quarterly*, Peter Marin argues that we safe, middle-class American types need uncivilized, savage people at our borders to teach us what life is really all about. "One thinks of Tolstoy among the Cossacks," he writes, "learning from the raw power of a life stripped clean of possessions and exposed to the rock-hard facts of the world. There was an austerity to their existence so pure that it became for him a kind of sensuality, and no doubt later in his life, when he wanted to strip himself morally to the bone, there was a similar element involved. There is a connection between moral power and the sense of exposure to the mortal elements and the feel of elements against the skin as you gallop a horse across the plain." The same species of connection I found, in those harshest and most simple of games.

True sanity revolves around these kinds of (dare I say it?) existentially pure acts: walking twenty waterless miles in the seashell dawn with a pebble beneath your tongue, sussing out the one gully in seven that leads to safety, etcetera, etcetera . . . And if we can't find border tribes to learn this stuff from—border tribes are having a hard time of it in this age—we must become our own border tribesmen and -women. (Recall Cavafy's words: "And now what shall become of us without the barbarians?/Those people were a kind of solution.") We must establish our own Outbacks and go out into them and bring the power there back into our everyday, "civilized" lives as portable lodestars to keep us on track through the vast unnatural inanity of the modern world. Those irrefutable truths, of sheer survival, life and death, have a way of keeping things in perspective.

Our ancestors, after all, spent three million years in a world as cruel and lucid as an ice crystal; they had little room for error, and it may have been that dire necessity which squeezed a kind of magic out of them, the same kind of magic we find in our lone games.

Lewis and Clark tell of a night, January 10, 1804, when the temperature at Fort Mandan in the Dakotas fell to −40°F.: "an Indian . . . who had . . . been missing returned to the fort, and although his dress was very thin, and he had slept on the snow without a fire, he had not suffered the slightest inconvenience." During the Second World War, U.S. Army doctors decided to test the resistance of Australian Aborigines to cold; they sent out a mixed party of American GIs and Abos into the outback in winter. Night fell. The Americans put on every stitch of clothing they had, stoked up the campfire, and did calisthenics around it all night to keep from freezing; the Aborigines took off their loincloths, rolled them up and put them behind their heads for pillows, lay down stark naked on the icy ground, and went to sleep. Every once in a while during the long and bitter night, one of the Aborigines would open an eye, look at the GIs leaping and capering and suffering, chuckle to himself, and go back to sleep.

I follow the stream down on the rocks, jumping like water on a griddle; a taste of that barebones ideation that transpires in the skull of the pinniped soaring at twenty-five miles an hour through the silver ice waters of the Arctic, or the snow leopard, eyes leaking furious light, bunching her muscles to leap. One California climber invented a sport, scree running, out of just such a revelation: he found that running alone down steep alpine rockfields brought him into a different, sharper level of consciousness. There was literally no time to make mistakes, and so no mistakes were made: leaping from tickle-point to razor's edge, over breakleg holes and hollows, without a moment's pause anywhere; he who hesitates is lost in these trickiest of dances.

One of the beauty parts of woods running is the way it mixes up disciplines and states of consciousness, depending on the terrain and one's response to it. Lope through woods; scramble down dodgy slopes; hop rocks, skate ice slicks; labor up steep hillsides, and, where they turn to near vertical rock, clamber and climb, air beneath your boot heels, trepidation rattling its cage in the back of your mind . . . A dialectic, flexing and unflexing, concentrating one's attention to the finest of fine points and then dispersing it to the winds.

I think we *Homo sapiens* lost something, some vital part of ourselves, when we gave up the hunting and gathering life for the fettered, programmed existence of agriculture, and later, industry. Consider just the moves: the lookout, the spoor, the stalk, the cross-country chase, the dead-on throw were replaced by the cramped, repetitive action of stoop labor, the planting stick and shovel, and worse, the quill, keyboard, and computer idiot stick. Time, which once rolled out in loose, measureless rounds of sun and moon, was chopped up into lengths and tied in knots; space, the free earth of the Paleolithic, was quartered and fenced: OFF LIMITS; TRES-PASSERS WILL BE PROSTITUTED.

And something in us died: mojo, obeah, mana, Buddha-hood, audacious rapture . . . dead. Dead and buried in an unmarked grave somewhere back there. Our ancestors knew more than we do: not only how to endure cold, blunt knives with their naked flesh, dance on pinpoints, but how to skin a flint, read buffalo in the flying scrolls of birds, whittle a flute out of your own fingerbone and play rain out of a dry sky on it . . . Poker players have known a flush beats a straight for over two hundred and fifty years, but the mathematics to prove it was only discovered a few years ago in complex cybernetic equations to the third decimal. How did the card players know? They just did, that's all.

It is this lost intuitive and powerful world that we contact in games like trekking, running, climbing, kayaking, hunting and fishing (sometimes), cross-country skiing (there is a two-thousand-year-old petroglyph of a skier on a cave wall in Norway), body surfing, even perhaps hang gliding (which is how early man *would have* flown if he had known how) . . . even, occasionally, mechanized and semi-mechanized sports like small-plane flying, sailing, and bicycling. Anything that gets us out alone into the preindustrial wild-ness, or a reasonable facsimile thereof, and then sticks it to us.

How else to explain the satisfaction climbers find muscling up some ghastly nameless rock spur in the foulest weather? To quote from Daumal's funny poem "The Lay of the Luckless Mountaineers":

Space itself has turned to sleet . . .
You know what I have? A memory block,
A stomach cramp, a flaming thirst,
And two fingers turned pale green.
We never did see the summit—
Except on the sardine can.
The rope jammed on every pull-through.
We passed a lifetime untangling the line,
And came to our senses with the cows in the dell.

"Have a good climb?"
"First rate. But tough."

Or the inscrutable satisfaction of hiking up a broiling ravine the color of stucco, with a too-heavy pack and bleeding feet, where the brush is thorny and the grass is doomed, and the water, if and when you find it, tastes like it came from Methuselah's bathtub? Or why I, one glorious winter, hitch-hiked an hour and a half up and back five days a week to ski boilerplate ice trails, on a pair of antique skis as heavy and thick as oars; so broke from paying for lift tickets that I lived for two solid weeks on popcorn, bouillon cubes, and scraps plucked from dirty plates in the ski area cafeteria?

There are endorphins and adrenalines, great leaps and visions . . . And then, on the outermost rim of things, are experiences that are just plain beyond the pale, so far out that they defy reason . . . but they can happen anyway.

I heard this story from a good friend of mine, an unimpeachable source whose name I will not use here. He had become interested in the possibilities of mountain running as a kind of meditation, and began doing long solo runs through the foothills west of Boulder, Colorado. He ran tough, going out for three, four, even six hours at a time, snow on the ground, in thunderstorms, over third- and fourth-class rock; after several months he felt like he was starting to get somewhere, that something might be getting ready to happen.

One day he was running on the Mesa Trail, through the meadows and woods below the Flatirons, those great tilted sandstone slabs that bulwark the easternmost foothills. He came to a small creek that ran down out of the rocks of Bear Mountain, and he paused and knelt to drink. As he drank, he found himself thinking of how the water came from the mountain, and how his drinking was a kind of communion with whatever spirit or strength resided up there. He decided suddenly to run up to the summit of Bear, up a hazardous trail he knew of that led up through the cliffs, steep and slick as a playground slide; he would run without stopping, as a kind of physical prayer to the peak, a ritual ordeal.

The nonstop run up the mountain was bitterly hard: his heart felt like it would burst; his knees collapsed; he grabbed on to trees and boulders to keep from falling. As he came out onto the stones of the mountaintop, he felt as if some kind of strange deal had been consummated between him and this piece of wilderness.

He stayed at the summit for a while, catching his breath, watching the afternoon sun change on the plains to the east, the forested hills to the west, leading to the snow peaks of the Divide along the far horizon.

Suddenly, several small sparrow hawks appeared around the mountaintop and began diving around him, so close that a couple of times he could feel the air blast from their wings. They wove around him, zooming away and then returning, again and again. He felt a sense of unease deep in the pit of his stomach; something was going on up there, not evil, but too much to deal with, he thought. Still he sat there, alone on the mountain, and watched the birds sail by.

The sparrow hawks flew away as abruptly as they had appeared. Then, from the four quarters of the sky, four ravens came flying; they approached the top of Bear Peak and then hovered in position, a hundred feet or so from where he stood: a hollow square, with him in the epicenter.

Still, he felt nothing malign in what was happening, only a sense that huge energies, invisible and implacable, were piling up all around him. He had drunk the wild water and made a promise; and now somehow a whole strange bargain had been made, it seemed. He began to descend the trail he had come up, picking his way down through the cliffs; but he had only gone a short distance when one of the black birds flew around in front of him and blocked his way, hanging there in the air, cawing at him. He climbed back up to the summit and waited to see what would happen next.

The ravens flew away, vanished. Then, far in the distance, he saw four tiny specks, flying toward him from the four points of the compass, just as the ravens had come. They coalesced into four red-tailed hawks, who approached until they were perhaps two hundred feet away; they too maneuvered there in position, almost stock-still in the sky, around him. After several minutes, they too flew away.

Then four enormous turkey vultures came out of the west, from over the mountains . . . but I will tell the rest of the story through the letter describing the incident he wrote me a couple of years later:

They remained in a stationary pattern for several minutes, and then glided down the mountain to the west. This was the closest I'd ever seen turkey vultures before, but I felt more numb and dazed than excited. Of course just before leaving again a shadow passed over me and I knew without looking that it was a golden eagle. It circled several times—again closer than I'd ever seen an eagle—and then went off I think to the southeast. By this time I was not in the observing mood and merely wanted to get down. As I left the peak I formed the hypothesis that there must be a dead animal somewhere near the top and that the birds had been attracted to it. I kept looking back in vain as I descended the mountain to see if any of the birds returned after I left. The glow in my stomach told me a different story, one I was not able to come to terms with until several weeks later.

Again, one does not know what to do with these kinds of stories, they are so far beyond our usual idea of things; but again, they do happen, whether we like it or not. I have heard plenty of other stories, on the extreme sports circuit, of what could only be called, for want of a better, cleaner word, miracles: the minatory ghost warning of danger just before an avalanche wipes the next pitch clean; the dream that comes true in midocean or at the dry waterhole or on black ice; the animal that appears at the precise and empty instant you need it to whisper in your ear. Recall the owls, that strange season, in the outbacks of the West.

What we are doing, without really meaning to, in our wild playing, is making a kind of religion: an incoherent, catch-as-catch-can kind of religion, but a religion nonetheless. It might have been Aldous Huxley who commented that modern man gets more visions and revelations in the dentist's chair (from nitrous oxide) than in the spiritless churches and synagogues of today. You could say the same thing of the more authentic experiences we find out on our "playing fields," the headwalls, pocket deserts, tundras, timberlands, seas, empty cinder tracks in the rain, factory walls*—all the wildernesses, great and small, where we play those primordial games: the connections we make out there are hallowed, through and through, religious in the deepest sense of the word.

I have been running nearly three hours now; running, jumping, climbing, slogging, the whole gamut. My breath streams out like smoke on the marble air; the old Adidas scuff up a black incense from the forest floor, the sepulchral humus beneath its cracked skin of frost. Fatigue's metallic flavor smolders on my tongue. If I stop for more than an instant, it will be all over: the knees will cramp up, the chill set in, and I will have to hobble the two plus miles back to the car like a game-legged mallard.

* Urban working-class climbers in Scotland and northern England have a sport sometimes called buildering, which consists of making ascents of man-made structures such as abandoned warehouses, highway overpasses, etc. The sport actually began at Oxford in the 1930s, when tipsy undergraduates began climbing clock towers and belfries by night; a guidebook was even published, of the best campus alpine routes. All of which goes to show that wilderness is where you find it.

Dusk is gathering, in this loneliest of hours: the river ice turns blue, and on the opposite shore, on the acier bluffs of Maryland, a few tender houselights have blossomed. A few miles south, downstream, the bridges will be stacked up with the rush-hour traffic: chains of headlights, leading out from the Iron Age capital and across the countryside.

I come to a point where I can choose one of two routes: a slog through thicket and sump that will take me down to the river again, or a climb up thirty-odd feet of cliff and then a couple of hundred feet of forty-five-degree woods back up onto the ridge. After a moment's hesitation, I take the latter: it is getting dark and cold, and I have miles to go to get back to the car.

My wet shoes skid on the smooth stone; fingers, numb with chill and weariness, seem to be operating at about 40 percent efficiency. And of course, as usual, I am an awful climber; the world-class California mountaineer Gordon Wiltsie once asked me if I wanted to do some huge, scarifying climb in the Sierras with him, and I told him, "I'm a Sherpa, not a climber." A porter, not a peak-bagger. I'll hump the load as far as Base Camp or Camp I, but someone else will have to take it from there.

About fifteen feet off the ground, it happens: I choose a poor handhold for my left hand, overreach with my right, and then my foot comes off all of a sudden and I half plummet, half slide to the bottom, landing with a crash in the brush. A twig snaps off, whipping back and stabbing me in the calf with the jagged end; a thin stream of blood shoots out. My fingertips burn, abraded on the rock. I clamber to my feet again, wrench myself from the thicket, and stagger on. I find a way around the cliff, a vitreous chute of dirt, ice, moss, and small stones, and somehow labor up it, using knees, nails, elbows, even my chin, for god's sake, in one place, to get a purchase. Well, heroism is seldom graceful, I tell myself; it's whatever works, whatever gets you through, that counts.

I climb up into the floor of the forest again, overlooking the river—darkness is coming on fast now, thickening in the branches, down in the hollows—and begin to run once more. From what I recall, it is about two and a half miles back to the car: twenty, twenty-five minutes, at the rate I am going. I weave through the timber and turn north on the first trail I hit; narrow, past a gleaming frozen puddle, through boulders, across a slumbering brook. Picking up speed, into a smooth, unraveling animal dance; the pain in my leg and fingers forgotten, the fatigue itself ebbing away, for the moment at least.

Even as the things around me—rocks, embankments, stumps, tree limbs, dry skeletal weeds, the creek water caroling in its hole—lose the last light of dusk, they seem to begin to incandesce, in some way I can't explain or describe, like objects seen through a night sniper's scope. As if someone had painted them with the dust of Australian opals. I can feel the power, impending; immanent; almost here again.

I run the last stretch of flat gravel trail through this strange enlightened night, flying the last half mile full tilt, nothing held back at all. There is the car, and I cross the last hundred feet of hard ground to it, hit the fender, and collapse across the hood.

I don't want to move, and I really couldn't even if I wanted to; not more than a few steps, anyway. I am suddenly conscious of the stabbing pain in my leg, where the stick pierced me, and the chilly perspiration against my skin, trapped by the heavy sweatshirt. The rusty salts of fatigue sting the corners of my eyes. I reach under the car, where I have hidden the car keys, unlock the door, and collapse inside into the driver's seat.

That light has vanished from the land; nothing but stark silhouettes out there now, with a musty glowing cloudbank above. That's all. I turn the key in the ignition, rev the motor, and turn the heater switch up all the way. Flick on the headlights, banishing the last fading vestiges of magic . . .

It is still out there; and I will be back.

Other Fromm Paperbacks:

KALLOCAIN: *A Novel*
by Karin Boye

AMERICAN NOTES: *A Journey*
by Charles Dickens

BEFORE THE DELUGE: *A Portrait of Berlin
in the 1920's*
by Otto Friedrich

J. ROBERT OPPENHEIMER: *Shatterer of Worlds*
by Peter Goodchild

THE ENTHUSIAST: *A Life of Thornton Wilder*
by Gilbert Harrison

INDIAN SUMMER: *A Novel*
by William Dean Howells

A CRACK IN THE WALL: *Growing Up Under Hitler*
by Horst Krüger

EDITH WHARTON: *A Biography*
by R. W. B. Lewis

THE CONQUEST OF MOROCCO:
by Douglas Porch

INTIMATE STRANGERS: *The Culture of Celebrity*
by Richard Schickel

KENNETH CLARK: *A Biography*
by Meryle Secrest

ALEXANDER OF RUSSIA: *Napoleon's Conqueror*
by Henri Troyat